THE COMMUNITY HOUSING HANDBOOK

In this book, readers journey through rural small towns to discover practical tools for driving meaningful change in housing. This book delves into the roots of present-day challenges of rural places, tracing their origins to shifts in economic and demographic landscapes. Chapters explore the pivotal role of housing for individuals and communities, shedding light on how small-town leaders often act only when prompted by crisis or opportunity. The authors furnish a blueprint outlining essential components for crafting and executing a housing strategy tailored to the unique needs of rural communities. The book culminates in a compelling call to action, coupled with a concise guide to best practices and common pitfalls in community housing efforts. It is ideal for community leaders and practitioners, and students in urban and regional planning as well as community development.

Kim Skobba is a Professor in the Housing Management and Policy program at the University of Georgia. Her research examines the relationship between housing and neighborhood conditions and the decision-making of community leaders in rural small towns, specifically examining how and why leaders address local housing needs.

Monica H. Callahan, Planning and Development Director for Madison, Georgia, is a nationally recognized expert in small-town planning, housing, and preservation. With 30 years of experience, she has led multimillion-dollar revitalization efforts, authored publications, and spoken at major conferences, shaping policy and infrastructure across the Southeast and beyond.

Jermaine M. Durham is an Associate Professor of Housing and Community Development at the University of Georgia and Director of the Georgia Initiative for Community Housing. In his multifaceted role, Durham seamlessly blends academic expertise with practical outreach, championing asset-based community development and spearheading locally driven housing initiatives.

THE COMMUNITY HOUSING HANDBOOK

Unlocking Housing Potential for Small Towns and Rural America

Kim Skobba, Monica H. Callahan, and Jermaine M. Durham

Routledge
Taylor & Francis Group
NEW YORK AND LONDON

Designed cover image: The Cottages On Vaughan in Clarkston, GA, built by The MicroLife Institute. Photo by The MicroLife Institute.

First published 2026
by Routledge
605 Third Avenue, New York, NY 10158

and by Routledge
4 Park Square, Milton Park, Abingdon, Oxon, OX14 4RN

Routledge is an imprint of the Taylor & Francis Group, an informa business

Library of Congress Cataloging-in-Publication Data
Names: Skobba, Kim author | Callahan, Monica H. author |
Durham, Jermaine M. author
Title: The community housing handbook: unlocking housing
potential for small towns and rural America / Kim Skobba,
Monica H. Callahan and Jermaine M. Durham.
Description: New York, NY: Routledge, 2026. |
Includes bibliographical references.
Identifiers: LCCN 2025052740 (print) | LCCN 2025052741 (ebook) |
ISBN 9781032859132 hardback | ISBN 9781032859125 paperback |
ISBN 9781003520450 ebook
Subjects: LCSH: Housing, Rural—United States |
Rural development—United States
Classification: LCC HD7289.U6 S56 2026 (print) | LCC HD7289.U6 (ebook)
LC record available at https://lccn.loc.gov/2025052740
LC ebook record available at https://lccn.loc.gov/2025052741

ISBN: 9781032859132 (hbk)
ISBN: 9781032859125 (pbk)
ISBN: 9781003520450 (ebk)

DOI: 10.4324/9781003520450

Typeset in Joanna
by codeMantra

For Dr. Karen Tinsley

CONTENTS

FOREWORD

Housing has always been more than shelter. It shapes the health, stability, and economic vitality of communities. Yet, for decades, many small towns and rural communities across America have faced housing challenges without the necessary resources and structured support to address them. *The community housing approach*, a framework modeled after the Georgia Initiative for Community Housing (GICH), offers a pathway forward for these communities.

We were honored to be part of the GICH program's early years, when the vision for a community-driven housing initiative was just getting started. Drawing from the lessons of the National League of Cities pilot, the Georgia Department of Community Affairs (DCA), Georgia Municipal Association, and University of Georgia's Housing and Demographics Research Center (now the Center for Housing and Community Research) formed a collaborative partnership, along with founding funder Georgia Power, to offer a similar program. Over the years, we have witnessed GICH evolve into a trusted model for housing capacity building, thanks to the leadership of state agencies, nonprofit partners, and community champions. We remain proud of the collaborative spirit that continues to drive the program's success.

Local governments play a vital role in the success of the GICH model, serving as conveners who bring diverse stakeholders together and sustain collaboration. As gatekeepers of policies such as zoning, land use, and code enforcement, they provide crucial political capital that makes housing initiatives more achievable and signals to the broader community that housing is a shared priority.

From its earliest days, GICH was designed not as a top-down solution but as a partnership with communities. The cohort model, in which teams of local leaders learn alongside one another over a three-year period, proved especially powerful. These local housing teams often included people who had not worked together, did not understand each other's points of view, or even trusted one another. The GICH program created spaces for candid conversations about housing challenges and opportunities and provided an accountability framework that allowed disparate groups to work together, set priorities, and pursue solutions to tough housing issues. The lessons learned in the early years of the GICH program were clear: every community faces housing challenges, but even the most deeply entrenched issues can be addressed when local leaders are given the tools, time, and support to take action.

Why does this matter for small towns? Unlike many larger urban communities, small towns often lack access to critical resources. Local leaders may not know where to start or how to address complex housing challenges. The community housing approach not only provides these communities with practical tools but also creates spaces where everyone—from school officials to housing authorities to local business leaders—can sit at the same table and take ownership of their community's housing future.

Since its inception, the GICH program has directly benefited more than 100 communities across Georgia. These communities represent a diverse mix of rural towns and urban areas, each with its own housing challenges and opportunities. A key component of the GICH has been the special benefits offered through the Georgia DCA, including access to the Community Development Block Grant (CDBG), the Community HOME Investment Program (CHIP), and the Low-Income Housing Tax Credit (LIHTC) program. These benefits have been instrumental in attracting over $475 million in housing and community development investments and nearly 14,000 LIHTC units in GICH communities.

This book matters because it goes beyond telling the story of the GICH and community housing approach. At its core, it provides a blueprint for rural and small-town communities across America to reclaim agency over their housing futures. It reminds us that solving housing challenges must be rooted in the local context, building strategic collaborations, proactive planning efforts, and leveraging social capital. It highlights that housing is not just a market issue but a human one. *The Community Housing Approach: Unlocking Housing Potential for Small Towns and Rural America* offers more than a model. It provides a blueprint for a movement rooted in partnership, accountability, and the belief that every community has the capacity to create housing solutions that serve its people.

Carmen Chubb, President, Colombia Residential and former Deputy Commissioner of Housing, Georgia Department of Community Affairs
Steve Foster, Retired, former Community Development Manager, Georgia Power
Thomas Rodgers, Professor Emeritus and former director of the Housing and Demographics Research Center, University of Georgia
Bill Thornton, Deputy Executive Director, Georgia Municipal Association

ACKNOWLEDGMENTS

As co-authors, we are grateful to the many individuals, communities, and institutions that have contributed to our understanding of community housing. Each of us brings distinct perspectives and experiences to bear, so here we offer gratitude both collectively and personally.

Respectfully, we would like to acknowledge the lasting contributions of Dr. Karen Tinsley, whose commitment to housing leadership development was felt throughout Georgia, by each of us, and is what made this book possible. Karen served as the program coordinator for the Georgia Initiative for Community Housing (GICH) from 2005 to 2018 and was the Director of the University of Georgia's (UGA) Housing and Demographic Research Center (now the Center for Housing and Community Research) at the time of her death in 2018. She was instrumental in launching the GICH program and was the driving force behind its success. For Karen, the GICH program was more than just a job—it was her life's mission. Her contributions to the community housing approach, including her research on the GICH model, resonate throughout the pages of this book.

We would also like to acknowledge the staff and leaders, past and present, of the GICH collaborative partnership, including the Georgia Department of Community Affairs, the Georgia Municipal Association, the UGA College of Family and Consumer Sciences, and founding sponsor Georgia Power. To local housing teams, advocates, and officials who granted their time and efforts to local initiatives and those who contributed to our research study—your lived experiences have informed our research and shaped the heart of this work. We also extend sincere appreciation to our reader group for their thoughtful guidance—Sarah Bellefuil, Matt Forshee, Chris Higdon, Carlos Tobar, and Jessica Tullar. Finally, we would like to thank Kate, Megha, Sarah, and Selena at Routledge for their encouragement and support throughout the writing and publishing process of this book.

I (Kim) am most grateful to my husband, Mike, for his thoughtful reading of early drafts, keeping my writing progress on track with his sticky note prowess, and his endless patience during the many weekends and evenings I spent holed up in my office writing this book. A special thank you to Mark Skobba for his perspective and assistance on numerous drafts, and to Mark Zvonkovic for his help in organizing the charts and graphs. I thank my UGA colleague, Dr. Jerry Shannon, for his many years of commitment to supporting GICH communities in collecting crucial housing assessment data, his research collaboration, and his service to the Center for Housing and Community Research. Finally, I thank my colleagues and students in the UGA Department of Financial Planning, Housing, and Consumer Economics and College of Family and Consumer Sciences for their encouragement and patience.

I (Jermaine) would like to acknowledge the pivotal leadership of the UGA College of Family and Consumer Sciences and the Center for Housing and Community Research, whose work continues to strengthen and inspire community housing efforts. My teaching and research are deeply enriched by opportunities to foster housing leadership, and I am profoundly grateful for the chance to help communities enter the housing arena with the skills and confidence to create lasting change. I also want to thank my parents, Mary Wilkins and Standford Durham, whose love, guidance, and unwavering belief in me have shaped both the man and the scholar I am today. Most importantly, I thank my amazing sons, Naim Durham and Kingston Durham, who are my constant source of joy, inspiration, and motivation to be a better person each day.

As local planning remains inherently proximate and political, I (Monica) am indebted to dedicated servant leaders—elected, employed, and appointed. Your wisdom, candor, and humor are community life preservers. Special thanks to my co-authors, peers, and friends for enduring my interactive, often iterative, problem-solving processes. For their unflagging support, I owe immeasurable gratitude to my parents, Wendell and Gloria Hobby, and to my sister, whom I love more. And above all my husband Ken Kocher - like Rilke's "guardian of my solitude" - is both my wellspring and my quiet harbor.

A deep sense of hopefulness sustains this work, rooted in the shared belief that equitable housing is both necessary and possible. Together, we extend a baton to civic leaders who are engaged, courageous, and undaunted. We hope you will take our community housing approach and run with it.

1

SETTING THE STAGE

HOUSING CHALLENGES AND COMMUNITY SOLUTIONS

Housing in small towns exists as a silent cornerstone, taken for granted amidst the ebb and flow of daily life. It only ever emerges from the shadows when a homebuilder develops a tract of land or when a troublesome rental property earns a code violation. For decades, this was how community leaders in Greenfield,[1] Georgia, a small town in the northeastern region of the state, thought about housing. Like many small towns, Greenfield's housing woes went unnoticed by local leaders aside from routine regulatory actions. That is, until distribution centers and significant economic development prospects materialized, prompted by its exurban location and proximity to an interstate highway. Among them was the possibility of an auto components factory, which would bring 2,500 jobs and lead to rapid population growth in this town of 6,500 residents. Sparked into action by the impending changes, community leaders began to take stock of their housing situation, quickly realizing that they faced a range of problems,

DOI: 10.4324/9781003520450-1

including a shortage of rental housing affordable to the workforce, limited options for prospective homebuyers, and an abundance of homes in substandard condition.

Across the state, a different scenario was unfolding in Pine Haven,[2] Georgia, an agricultural community with a population of about 3,000 residents in the southeastern part of the state. Pine Haven is located about an hour south of Augusta, Georgia, a mid-sized city best known for hosting the prestigious Masters golf tournament. Despite its proximity to Augusta, the conditions in Pine Haven were worlds away from the affluence and glamour of this internationally acclaimed event. Instead, Pine Haven reflected the struggling housing and economic development conditions facing many small towns in the U.S. The town was hit hard by the collapse of the U.S. textile industry in the early 2000s and the subsequent Great Recession. Major employers left, leaving few employment opportunities for residents. By 2020, Pine Haven had lost 25% of its population from its peak of 4,000 residents two decades earlier. The community struggled to diversify its local economy. Community leaders saw tourism and retiree attraction as ways to boost their economy. However, housing problems and co-occurring quality-of-life issues, which fell below the standard required to attract new people and businesses, were obstacles to their economic development aspirations. Over one-third of Pine Haven's rental property was dilapidated. Only a handful of new housing units have been built in the past decade, contributing to a limited range of options for new and existing residents. Despite weak economic conditions, the community faced housing affordability issues similar to those of economically thriving small towns, such as Greenfield, Georgia.

The housing problems found in Greenfield and Pine Haven are common across rural America. From Seaside, Oregon to Radford, Virginia, news stories citing rural housing shortages and affordability challenges are becoming commonplace. These stories align with research indicating that housing cost burden, which occurs when households spend more than 30% of their income on housing costs, has increased significantly among rural households over the past two decades (Housing Assistance Council, 2023). Over 40% of rural renters and nearly one-fifth of rural homeowners live in housing that costs too much compared to their incomes (Housing Assistance Council, 2023; Joint Center for Housing Studies of Harvard University, 2023). The lack of funding for new affordable rental housing,

Figure 1.1 Old house.

Photo credit: Cal Powell, University of Georgia College of Family and Consumer Sciences.

combined with insufficient resources to preserve existing affordable rentals, has created a deficit while exacerbating the affordability crisis in rural America (Scally, Gilbert, et al., 2018).

Why Do Critical Housing Issues Go Unaddressed?

Ask why housing problems exist, and you will likely hear many explanations. Economists will point out that housing problems in small towns are a function of basic economics. In a private market, supply and demand drive housing quantities and prices. Increased demand should lead to greater supply. However, this principle often does not hold for housing, especially in rural housing markets (Local Housing Solutions, 2025). If you ask residents of small towns with thriving tourism-based economies, you may hear that the private market response to increased housing demand has not fixed the community's housing problems. Perhaps housing problems persist in rural areas due to a shortage of people and housing expertise? Yes, addressing housing issues does require capacity within the community (and money!) (Scally, Gilbert, et al., 2018). Community leaders in places like Pine Haven, Georgia, may tell you that their community's housing issues are overlooked in favor of those in large cities. Yes, most policies and funding for housing are directed toward urban areas, leaving rural communities out of the conversation (Ajilore & Willingham, 2020). This invisibility of rural communities in federal housing policy may be particularly apparent if you live in or near an American Indian or Alaskan native community (Dewees & Marks, 2017; Gavazzi, 2023; U.S. Government Accountability Office, 2024). Finally, if you are learning that small towns and rural areas have significant housing problems, it may be due to lingering misperceptions that these communities have an ample supply of reasonably priced housing, which has made recognition of the problem more challenging (Mathur, 2016; Scally, Gilbert, et al., 2018). While all of the circumstances above are contributing factors, they are not the reason issues persist in small towns.

Why do small towns have lingering housing problems? While the issues highlighted above are factors, we argue that housing problems persist in small towns and rural areas because addressing local housing needs has not been included on the list of responsibilities for most community leaders. Rural and small-town local governments have limited their role in housing to regulation and code enforcement, rather than actively engaging in community-based decision-making and action around housing. This approach to housing means that for most small towns, the responsibility of housing is left to private market homebuilders, housing developers, and landlords.

Most small towns are not proactive when it comes to housing. Sure, some may have an active housing authority or a nonprofit housing organization providing housing or services. While these organizations offer some relief to low- and moderate-income residents, segments of the housing shortage are not addressed by these organizations. These crucial housing types include workforce housing and missing middle housing, which include small-scale apartment buildings, duplexes, triplexes, and cottage courts. Eventually, the gap between the community's existing housing and the housing it needs becomes so large that it becomes impossible to ignore. The relatively few communities that have taken a proactive approach to housing stand out from the rest. We highlight several of these communities in this book.

Leaving the responsibility of housing entirely to the private market works until it doesn't. It ultimately falters because the profit incentive of developers and landlords results in servicing only some segments of the population, substandard rental housing, or ignoring rural communities altogether. At some point, this gap becomes large enough to cause a problem. In towns like Pine Haven, leaving housing decisions to the private market mostly worked while the local economy was strong. When economic conditions eroded, homebuilders and developers left along with employers and jobs. With limited options for homebuyers and a visible prevalence of dilapidated housing, local leaders in Pine Haven recognized that improving the community's housing was critical to its economic future. For Greenfield, a hands-off approach to housing resulted in an abundance of poor-quality rental housing, most of which was owned by out-of-state landlords. Despite poor conditions, rental housing was not affordable for many households in the community. Homeowners also experienced significant housing affordability challenges. Faced with residents' concerns about quality of life, impending economic development, population growth, and mounting housing problems, Greenfield's community leaders recognized that ignoring issues was no longer an option. We have labeled this moment of reckoning the *Eureka Moment*. Based on our research, experience working with communities, and the increasing number of news stories highlighting the rural housing crisis, we know that many small-town leaders and community members across the country have reached this moment of reckoning.

This book introduces a new way forward—the community housing approach. Drawing on our experience with community housing initiatives through our work as planners, researchers, and housing practitioners. In the following few chapters, we will make the case for why deferring decisions about housing to the private market is not sustainable for rural communities over the long term and why the community housing approach is needed to address the housing challenges facing these small towns across the U.S. This does not mean we are anti-private market housing. It is just the opposite. Homebuilders, developers, and landlords are critical partners. Housing programs and incentives often rely on private developers and landlords to participate in much-needed housing efforts. However, the private market does not shoulder any responsibility for the well-being and prosperity of the community. It is motivated by market needs rather than community needs. The private market is unlikely to appear when your community is in economic decline and faces housing challenges that require solutions.

Finding Solutions Within: Introducing the Community Housing Approach

Community leaders can play a crucial role in fostering vibrant and sustainable housing solutions if they are proactive in planning for housing that meets the needs of both current and future residents. And, as the title of this book suggests, we are offering the community housing approach as a model to guide rural communities. The approach is community-driven, utilizing a dedicated team of local stakeholders who implement a process of assessment, planning, and action that is focused on providing the housing that the community wants and needs. The community housing approach represents a transformational strategy that addresses the housing needs of current and future residents by encouraging a pivotal shift in the mindset of community leaders. Rather than viewing housing challenges through a reactive lens, this strategy promotes a proactive, locally led initiative that emphasizes collaboration, data-driven solutions, and the active involvement of local leaders. By fostering a sense of shared responsibility and collective action, the community housing approach addresses the immediate housing needs of residents and the long-term vitality and resiliency of communities. This strategy exemplifies how local leaders can serve as powerful catalysts for change, transforming how communities address housing challenges (Mattessich & Monsey, 1997; Phillips & Pittman, 2015).

This book's blueprint for community housing is the result of decades of community-led housing change. We draw on our collective decades of experience studying and working alongside communities as they solve their housing challenges; however, the approach we share here is not our invention. The community housing approach is a proven blueprint forged by the program partners and communities participating in the Georgia Initiative for Community Housing (GICH), a statewide program launched in 2005 following participation in a similarly structured National League of Cities pilot program.

The GICH program provides the model for the community housing approach. The program supports cities and counties in developing housing work plans tailored to their unique needs. Over three years, participating communities benefit from educational resources, peer learning opportunities, and networking events designed to bolster their housing-related knowledge and social capital. A key component of the program is the formation of a housing team that reflects a broad cross-section of the community, ensuring a diverse range of perspectives and expertise at the table. These teams engage in a collaborative planning and implementation process, guided by facilitators who help translate objectives into actionable strategies.

The community housing approach, GICH, and the former National League of Cities pilot program are all grounded in community development principles that focus on enhancing the collective capacity of local leaders and stakeholders to foster positive change within their communities (Green & Haines, 2016). At the heart of the approach is the critical role that social capital—the value derived from social networks and relationships—plays in achieving housing and economic development goals (Putnam, 1993). Social capital facilitates the mobilization of resources, ideas, and information, enabling communities to leverage

Figure 1.2 MicroLife Institute Cottage Court Development.

Source: MicroLife Institute.

these assets to address their housing needs (Chaskin, 2001). This concept underscores the importance of building strong, trust-based relationships among community members, local businesses, nonprofit organizations, and government entities. By doing so, communities can tap into a broader spectrum of resources and opportunities, extending their impact well beyond the local level.

Over the following chapters, we will take a deeper look at the housing challenges rural communities encounter, the reasons behind these challenges, and what small-town leaders can do to start solving housing problems. We then provide a model for community housing, drawing on our combined decades of experience working on and studying housing, small-town planning, and decision-making. We will map out the essential components that local leaders need to make housing happen in their communities.

Why Rural and Small-Town Housing Matters—What's at Stake

Taking a proactive approach to housing requires change, and we all know change is hard. The community housing approach requires building capacity within the community. It requires bringing people together who may not be in the same social circles or share the same views. Researching, understanding the problem, and creating a plan for moving forward takes time and effort. It also requires a change of perspective that views housing as a community resource and a form of infrastructure that requires attention and resources. Changing the perspectives of community leaders and residents in this way can be challenging, especially if their beliefs or experiences have led them to believe that government involvement in housing often yields bad outcomes. While these changes may require time, effort, and adjustments, it is worth the investment. Housing is pivotal to the well-being of residents and the economic vitality of your community. We invite you to consider the following ways in which housing matters:

Affordable housing is a powerful economic driver. Having housing options that are affordable to a range of residents will give your community a strategic advantage in the fiercely competitive economic development landscape. Housing availability and affordability are key factors in the decision-making process for businesses (Leigh & Blakely, 2017; Scally, Dabir, et al.,

2018; Wardrip et al., 2011). While a supply of affordable housing options provides a competitive edge in economic development, a shortage can impede overall economic growth (Anthony, 2023; Lubell, 2023). Bringing affordable housing development to your community has the added benefit of boosting local spending, which supplies more revenue for your local government (Wardrip et al., 2011).

Housing is a critical factor in nurturing and retaining a local workforce. In addition to improving your community's economic development prospects, the availability of workforce housing directly benefits local employers by increasing employee reliability and retention rates. Greater housing variety makes attracting and retaining talent at all job levels easier. Research indicates that a lack of reasonably priced housing disrupts workforce stability, while the presence of workforce housing is linked to improved employment prospects for residents (Davies, 2018; Fritts, 2020; Saraswat, 2021). Developing new housing, particularly multifamily housing, generates employment opportunities during construction and in post-development operations (Kane et al., 2022).

Housing serves as a cornerstone for residents' well-being and prosperity. Everyone in your community needs a place to live. Housing in good condition and affordable relative to household income is essential to residents' well-being. When people in your community pay too much for housing, it limits their resources for other basic needs, including healthcare, transportation, and adequate nutrition (Airgood-Obrycki et al., 2023; Meyers et al., 2005). For children in your community, living in stable, high-quality housing is particularly important, given its positive impact on their physical, social-emotional health, and educational outcomes (Gensheimer et al., 2022; Harkness & Newman, 2005). Living in affordable housing during childhood is associated with increased earnings and facilitates adults' educational and professional growth (Derby, 2021; Reid, 2018). Affordable housing tools—particularly rent subsidies and increased supply of income-restricted homes—are linked to reduced displacement and overcrowding, which strengthens overall community well-being (Schapiro et al., 2022; Wood et al., 2008).

Proactively addressing your community's housing needs will extend beyond improved housing. Your efforts will provide residents with the stability and resilience needed to thrive and a foundation for economic growth and advancement. They will provide a return on your investment that benefits the community through resident satisfaction, the ability to meet basic needs, and collective well-being (Flora et al., 2016; Green & Haines, 2016).

Housing serves as an equity tool in rural communities. Adequate and affordable housing ensures that vulnerable neighbors—seniors, low-income families, and people with disabilities—can remain in their hometowns with dignity and stability (Okoye et al., 2025; Vega & Wallace, 2016). Offering a mix of housing options can help to correct long-standing imbalances and ensure that historically underserved groups can thrive. Black and Indigenous communities in the rural U.S. still live with the legacy of dispossession, discriminatory practices, and unequal access to mortgage credit (Dyer & Bailey, 2008; Geisler, 2014; Mann & Rogers, 2021). Well-designed affordable housing strategies can begin to repair these inequities by opening paths to homeownership, protecting intergenerational wealth, and preventing land loss.

What Makes a Place Rural or a Small Town? It Depends on Who You Ask

This book uses the terms rural, small town, and rural community interchangeably. What do we mean by these terms? Rural definitions are numerous and varied, but typically include some combination of geography, population, and housing. For example, the U.S. Census Bureau (2020) defines rural areas as open land and communities with fewer than 2,000 housing units or 5,000 residents. The U.S. Department of Agriculture's Economic Research Service (2024) employs a different approach, using Rural-Urban Continuum Codes to classify counties on a scale from 1 (large metro area) to 9 (completely rural).

Like rural definitions, there's little agreement on what makes a place a small town. Definitions vary widely, ranging from a place with fewer than 5,000 people to one with up to 50,000. Some definitions also include a place's physical characteristics, such as a compact, self-contained community set apart from a major urban area (Wuthnow, 2013). However, ask someone in America to define a small town, and they are more likely to give you a cultural image than a population number. This image often includes a main street with independent businesses, walkable in-town neighborhoods, and well-kept single-family homes. The social characteristics are equally important: a place where everyone knows everyone, neighbors are supportive, and the pace of life is slower and distinct from that of a big city (Hummon, 1990). This idyllic view is easily found in popular culture, from the Hallmark movie channel to TV shows like *Gilmore Girls* or movies like *Pleasantville*.

What makes a place a rural or small town is often a matter of interpretation rather than a clear definition. Instead of adding to the long list of existing definitions, we leave that determination to you, the reader. If you consider your community a small town in a rural area, it is. Below, we offer a set of community characteristics that align with who we think will most likely benefit from reading this book. These characteristics share aspects of rural and small-town definitions, but include other features we have identified through our work with communities in Georgia.

- **Your community's local government has limited staff dedicated to housing**. You may have an economic development director working on housing, but this is a part of the job rather than the whole job. Without housing staff, your community may rely on guidance from outside sources, typically state, regional, nonprofit staff, or consulting resources for housing expertise.
- **Your community lacks the capacity and access to resources to address housing**. This characteristic is related to the lack of human capital but goes beyond just staffing. Funding for housing in the U.S. is largely targeted toward urban areas and the networks of housing expertise common in large metropolitan areas. Rural and small towns are often disconnected from these networks.
- **Your community's population size and/or proximity to an urban area limit your ability to address housing**. The size or distance from a major city is a factor, but only as it relates to constraining community capacity and access to resources.

What to Expect

Over the following 11 chapters, we embark on a journey into small towns that will equip you with indispensable tools to cultivate meaningful change. This book begins by digging into the roots of the present-day challenges of rural places, tracing their origins to shifts in economic and demographic landscapes. We explore the pivotal role of housing for individuals and communities, highlighting the tendency of small-town leaders to address housing only when a crisis or opportunity compels reaction. After this, we furnish a comprehensive blueprint outlining the essential components for crafting and executing a housing strategy that caters to the unique needs of rural communities. We conclude with a final chapter that offers a compelling call to action and a concise compendium of best practices and potential stumbling blocks encountered on the path to improved community housing.

This book draws upon our collective research and work as practitioners with rural communities. We rely on our research, which includes case studies of small towns in Georgia actively working to address local housing problems and interviews with community leaders of housing initiatives outside of Georgia. We use pseudonyms for communities involved in research studies as part of our research Appendix. The case study research is augmented by case examples, based on news stories and publicly available information, from small towns in other parts of the U.S. We use the actual names for these communities. In addition to case study research, we include findings from two statewide surveys on the housing needs of communities across Georgia. We also draw on our professional experiences supporting rural small-town housing planning and working with the GICH program, a statewide housing technical assistance program led by the University of Georgia's College of Family and Consumer Sciences' Center for Housing and Community Research, in partnership with the Georgia Department of Community Affairs, Georgia Municipal Association, and Georgia Power.

In the following chapters, we will highlight the critical implications for communities and their residents when leaders fail to address housing needs proactively. Most books and resources about housing focus on urban centers and larger cities with dedicated housing staff, established planning departments, and policy experts. In this book, we focus on housing in rural communities. The overarching problems of affordability, adequacy, and supply in cities large and small, urban and rural, are often similar. Yet the solutions for small towns and rural places are different. These communities usually do not have the luxury of hiring expertise; instead, they must cultivate it. The *community housing approach* emphasizes the indispensable role of local leaders and provides practical tools that foster vibrant and sustainable small towns.

If you are a student or a nascent housing practitioner, we hope this book will aid your understanding of how to tackle housing challenges in rural and small-town areas, adding to the limited academic work addressing this topic. We hope this book will not only serve as a valuable resource but will also broaden the discourse among affordable housing and planning academicians and experts, transcending urban boundaries and offering a more comprehensive examination of housing challenges and viable pathways for solving these problems.

Whether you are a present or future community leader or a practitioner responsible for addressing local housing problems within small towns, reading this book will provide practical information to help you on your journey toward more and better housing. Through our research and experience working with communities, we know small-town leaders have their Eureka Moment when they realize the private market is not going to solve their housing problems. In this book, we offer a path forward after this a-ha moment. However, we would like to convince you to use the community housing approach before the hurricane hits, the large plant locates nearby, or the young families you would like to have as residents move elsewhere. Whether before or after a Eureka Moment, we will provide you with a strategic blueprint to make housing happen in your community.

Notes

1 Greenfield is a pseudonym. See Appendix for more information.
2 Pine Haven is a pseudonym. See Appendix for more information.

References

Abt Associates, & NYU Furman Center. (2026). Local Housing Solutions. https://www.localhousingsolutions.org

Airgood-Obrycki, W., Hermann, A., & Wedeen, S. (2023). "The Rent Eats First": Rental housing unaffordability in the United States. *Housing Policy Debate*, 33(6), 1272–1292. https://doi.org/10.1080/10511482.2021.2020866

Ajilore, O., & Willingham, C. Z. (2020). *The path to rural resilience in America*. Center for American Progress. https://www.americanprogress.org/article/path-rural-resilience-america/

Anthony, J. (2023). Housing affordability and economic growth. *Housing Policy Debate*, 33(5), 1187–1205. https://doi.org/10.1080/10511482.2022.2065328

Chaskin, R. J. (2001). Building community capacity: A definitional framework and case studies from a comprehensive community initiative. *Urban Affairs Review, 36*(3), 291–323. https://doi.org/10.1177/10780870122184876

Davies, P. (2018). Houses are where jobs sleep at night. *Federal Reserve Bank of Minneapolis.* https://www.minneapolisfed.org/article/2018/houses-are-where-jobs-sleep-at-night

Derby, E. (2021). Does growing up in tax-subsidized housing lead to higher earnings and educational attainment? *SSRN Electronic Journal.* https://doi.org/10.2139/ssrn.3491787

Dewees, S., & Marks, B. (2017). *Twice invisible: Understanding rural Native America* (No. 2; Research Note). First Nations Development Institute.

Dyer, J. F., & Bailey, C. (2008). A place to call home: Cultural understandings of heir property among Rural African Americans. *Rural Sociology, 73*(3), 317–338. https://doi.org/10.1526/003601108785766598

Flora, C. B., Flora, J. L., & Gasteyer, S. P. (2016). *Rural communities: Legacy and change* (Fifth edition). Westview Press.

Fritts, L. (2020). Affordable housing: A key element of economic development. *Partnership for Housing Affordability.* https://pharva.com/project/affordable-housing-a-key-element-of-economic-development/

Gavazzi, S. M. (2023). Emerging ideas: The near invisibility of Native Americans and their families within the flagship journals of family science. *Family Relations, 72*(3), 923–931. https://doi.org/10.1111/fare.12650

Geisler, C. (2014). Disowned by the ownership society: How Native Americans lost their land. *Rural Sociology, 79*(1), 56–78. https://doi.org/10.1111/ruso.12028

Gensheimer, S. G., Eisenberg, M. D., Hindman, D., Wu, A. W., & Pollack, C. E. (2022). Examining health care access and health of children living in homes subsidized by the Low-Income Housing Tax Credit. *Health Affairs, 41*(6), 883–892. https://doi.org/10.1377/hlthaff.2021.01806

Green, G. P., & Haines, A. (2016). *Asset building & community development* (Fourth edition). SAGE.

Harkness, J., & Newman, S. J. (2005). Housing affordability and children's well-being: Evidence from the national survey of America's families. *Housing Policy Debate, 16*(2), 223–255. https://doi.org/10.1080/10511482.2005.9521542

Housing Assistance Council. (2023). *Taking stock.* Housing Assistance Council. https://takingstockrural.org/taking-stock/

Hummon, D. M. (1990). *Commonplaces: Community ideology and identity in American culture.* State University of New York Press.

Joint Center for Housing Studies of Harvard University. (2023). *The state of the nation's housing 2023.* Harvard University.

Kane, S., Durham, J., Skobba, K., & Shannon, J. (2022). *Revisiting the economic impact of Low-Income Housing Tax Credits in Georgia.* University of Georgia. https://www.fcs.uga.edu/docs/LIHTC-Economic-Impact-022223-Digital.pdf

Leigh, N. G., & Blakely, E. J. (2017). *Planning local economic development: Theory and practice* (Sixth edition). SAGE.

Lubell, J. (2023, August 14). *Deconstructing the national housing dilemma.* National Conference of State Legislatures Legislative Summit, Indianapolis, IN. https://documents.ncsl.org/wwwncsl/Summit/2023/Session-Resources/Lubell-Presentation-to-NCSL-Conference_2023_08_10-FINAL.pdf

Mann, B., & Rogers, A. (2021). Segregation now, segregation tomorrow, segregation forever? Racial and economic isolation and dissimilarity in rural Black Belt schools in Alabama. *Rural Sociology*, 86(3), 523–558. https://doi.org/10.1111/ruso.12384

Mathur, S. (2016). Are renters and homeowners in rural areas cost-burdened? *Housing Perspectives (Joint Center for Housing Studies of Harvard University)*. https://www.jchs.harvard.edu/blog/are-renters-and-homeowners-in-rural-areas-cost-burdened

Mattessich, P., & Monsey, B. (1997). *Community building: What makes it work*. Amherst H. Wilder Foundation.

Meyers, A., Cutts, D., Frank, D. A., Levenson, S., Skalicky, A., Heeren, T., Cook, J., Berkowitz, C., Black, M., Casey, P., & Zaldivar, N. (2005). Subsidized housing and children's nutritional status: Data from a multisite surveillance study. *Archives of Pediatrics & Adolescent Medicine*, 159(6), 551. https://doi.org/10.1001/archpedi.159.6.551

Okoye, S. M., Samuel, L. J., Fabius, C. D., Ortiz, K., Pollack, C. E., Gitlin, L. N., Szanton, S. L., & Wolff, J. L. (2025). Housing characteristics of low and moderate income older adults with and without disabilities. *Geriatric Nursing*, 62, 175–181. https://doi.org/10.1016/j.gerinurse.2025.01.042

Phillips, R., & Pittman, R. H. (Eds.). (2015). *An introduction to community development* (Second edition). Routledge.

Putnam, R. D. (1993). What makes democracy work? *National Civic Review*, 82(2), 101–107. https://doi.org/10.1002/ncr.4100820204

Reid, C. K. (2018). *The links between affordable housing and economic mobility: The experiences of residents living in Low-Income Housing Tax Credit properties*. Terner Center for Housing Innovation, UC Berkeley. https://ternercenter.berkeley.edu/wp-content/uploads/2020/08/Links_Between_Affordable_Housing_and_Economic_Mobility_.pdf

Saraswat, D. (2021). Labor market impacts of exposure to affordable housing supply: Evidence from the Low-Income Housing Tax Credit program. *SSRN Electronic Journal*. https://doi.org/10.2139/ssrn.4059439

Scally, C. P., Dabir, S., & Lipsetz, D. (2018). National rural housing policy and programs: Opportunities and challenges. In Albrecht, D. E., Loveridge, S., Goetz, S., & Welborn, R. (Eds.), *Rural housing and economic development* (pp. 88–107). Routledge.

Scally, C. P., Gilbert, B., Hedman, C., Gold, A., & Posey, L. (2018). *Rental housing for a 21st century rural America*. Urban Institute. https://www.urban.org/research/publication/rental-housing-21st-century-rural-america

Schapiro, R., Blankenship, K., Rosenberg, A., & Keene, D. (2022). The effects of rental assistance on housing stability, quality, autonomy, and affordability. *Housing Policy Debate*, 32(3), 456–472. https://doi.org/10.1080/10511482.2020.1846067

U.S. Census Bureau. (2020). *Understanding and using American Community Survey data: What users of data for rural areas need to know*. U.S. Census Bureau.

U.S. Department of Agriculture Economic Research Service. (2024). *Rural-Urban Continuum Codes documentation*. https://www.ers.usda.gov/data-products/rural-urban-continuum-codes/documentation/

U.S. Government Accountability Office. (2024). *Tribal issues: Barriers to access to federal assistance* (No. GAO-25–107674). https://www.gao.gov/products/gao-25-107674

Vega, W. A., & Wallace, S. P. (2016). Affordable housing: A key lever to community health for older Americans. *American Journal of Public Health*, 106(4), 635–636. https://doi.org/10.2105/AJPH.2015.303034

Wardrip, K., Williams, L., & Hague, S. (2011). *The role of affordable housing in creating jobs and stimulating local economic development: A review of the literature*. Center for Housing Policy. https://www.opportunityhome.org/wp-content/uploads/2018/02/Housing-and-Economic-Development-Report-2011.pdf

Wood, M., Turnham, J., & Mills, G. (2008). Housing affordability and family well-being: Results from the housing voucher evaluation. *Housing Policy Debate, 19*(2), 367–412. https://doi.org/10.1080/10511482.2008.9521639

Wuthnow, R. (2013). *Small-town America*. Princeton University Press.

2

UNRAVELING THE PAST TO IMPROVE HOUSING FOR THE FUTURE

Tracing demographic, economic, and social changes in rural America over the past 150 years provides valuable insight into today's housing context in these communities. If you are a history buff, you will likely embrace this journey. If just thinking about history makes your eyes glaze over and you're tempted to skip ahead, we urge you to stay with us. Many beliefs and actions shaping housing in small towns today are intertwined with the past. Having a clear understanding of the historical context that has influenced your community's present-day challenges and beliefs about housing solutions is necessary when planning for change. Understanding the historical context may make the difference between a housing plan that works and one that is quickly discarded. If you are ready to work on solutions, this book's early chapters may seem like the equivalent of fly-over states—the place between where you are and where you want to be. Yet, as with fly-over places, we believe exploring these foundational chapters will be worth your time.

DOI: 10.4324/9781003520450-2

So, let's start at the beginning. To understand today's housing challenges, we need to look at where small towns came from and how the way of life in these communities developed and changed over time.

The Historical Context of Rural America

Small Towns, the Early Years

The U.S. began as a country of small towns. Across the country, small towns shared two key features: (1) they depended on resource-based industries like agriculture, fishing, forestry, and mining, and (2) they were largely self-sufficient in meeting their food and housing needs (Albrecht, 2007). The outline of small towns of the past persists in quaint main streets with locally owned shops, diners, a post office, and a town hall, often in buildings imbued with historic or vintage charm. Main streets serve as a reminder of the growth and prosperity of early industrialization made possible through innovation. The invention of the steam engine brought railroad networks linking small towns to urban industrial centers, powering factories that produced commodities, generating demand for the rich natural resources found in rural communities. Access to lumber and the advent of factories that produced millwork made it possible for Victorian-era homes with gingerbread trim ubiquitous in small towns across the U.S. Main streets bustled with local businesses. Farmers produced cash crops, mining towns generated coal, and textile mills provided material for consumer goods. For small towns, a stop on the railroad network meant connections to other people and places, new thriving businesses, and a population boom supporting the development of a central downtown district and new, in-town housing. Rural America's small towns were self-reliant and thriving (Albrecht, 2007).

Small towns, however, were not the only places experiencing change from the transportation revolution. The number of cities proliferated along with the urban population, as innovations in transportation increased the demand for urban manufacturing and a workforce to support it (Atack et al., 2022). Increasing urbanization in the U.S. and abroad fostered social distinctions between small towns and big cities. In 1887, German sociologist Ferdinand Tönnies (1988) published the book *Gemeinschaft and Gesellschaft* (translated as *Community and Society*), suggesting that industrialization created societal changes reflected in distinctly different social relationships in urban and rural places. *Gemeinschaft* (community) represented the social bonds formed in rural communities through a commonality of kinship, locality, and emphasis on cooperation. *Gesellschaft* (society), in contrast, represented relationships based on competition, wealth, and control formed in cities amidst urbanization and modernization. The stereotypical city was an impersonal place plagued by decline, physically run-down neighborhoods, and crime; small towns were warm, neighborly places, offering equality and the good life (Jakle, 1999). These distinctions likely resonated in the U.S. as urbanization brought concerns over a declining way of life (Hibbard & Frank, 2021). As economic and demographic shifts have transformed rural communities, the social identities and emotional connections to these places remain strong even though most people in the U.S. now reside in urban areas (Kley & Paul, 2015). Social characteristics like community-mindedness, cooperation, loyalty, and hard work remain closely associated with beliefs about small-town life (Hibbard & Frank, 2021). These social characteristics can be leveraged to address community housing and other modern-day challenges, yet the idealized attributes of small towns can also lead to complacency.

Post-World War II to the 1970s: Rural Industrialization

Despite persistent beliefs about geographic differences, the gap between rural and urban life was narrowing. By the 1950s, rural residents watched the same TV shows and read the same newspapers as residents in large cities. Transportation between small towns and big cities became easier, providing rural residents greater access to nearby cities than in previous decades. Yet a transformation was underway. The number of farms and farmworkers declined due to technology improvements that enabled more efficient and extensive farm operations, prompting moves by rural residents to urban areas for employment (Albrecht, 2007; Beale, 1993). At the same time, transportation improvements made it possible for rural communities to attract manufacturing jobs (Albrecht, 2007). This change marked the beginning of several waves of changes that would profoundly impact rural populations' economic and social well-being (Falk & Lobao, 2003). Economic restructuring changed how the rural economy worked—from the kinds of jobs available, to relationships between people, employers, and government—influencing whether places thrived or struggled (Falk & Lobao, 2003). Changes hit small towns especially hard because they had fewer people, less diverse economies, lower income levels, and lower levels of education and skills. This process and its effects on people, jobs, and communities still shape challenges facing many rural communities today, including housing challenges.

Following World War II, rural communities experienced economic growth, even as the population of Americans in rural areas declined. American agriculture was changing rapidly, with technological advances increasingly replacing human labor and agribusiness replacing the family farm (Buttel, 2003). These changes left farmers in need of other or additional employment options. Manufacturing jobs filled this role by providing jobs for people with high school diplomas, a source of nonfarm income, and higher wages and benefits than other jobs available in rural areas (Green, 2020; Green & Sanchez, 2007). Post-World War II manufacturing filled the demand for consumer goods, supporting the rise of homeownership and an increased standard of living in the country, which was due in part to rising incomes from the unionization of manufacturing jobs that lifted overall wage levels (Falk & Lobao, 2003). Manufacturing jobs appeared as car ownership increased, making it possible for rural residents to drive a distance to nonfarm employment (Warren, 2014). Local governments began using economic development tools to attract these jobs by offering incentives, tax concessions, local industrial bond financing, and statewide and local development credit corporations (Warren, 2014).

Manufacturing helped many rural communities gain in population and jobs. Yet, people with lower incomes and levels of education were less likely to benefit from economic activity (Falk & Lobao, 2003). As populations increased in these communities, so did the demand for housing, adversely affecting people with lower incomes (Falk & Lobao, 2003; Ziebarth & Tigges, 2003). Industrialized agriculture emerged alongside manufacturing, resulting in larger but fewer farms, population loss due to out-migration, and lower levels of rural economic well-being as poverty and unemployment rose without adequate community services to support these needs (Falk & Lobao, 2003).

1970s to Early 1990s: Farm Crisis and Shift to Manufacturing and Service Jobs

Rural communities witnessed a tremendous boom followed by a steep decline in the following decades. While U.S. farms experienced a precipitous drop in numbers between the 1930s and the early 1970s, farms

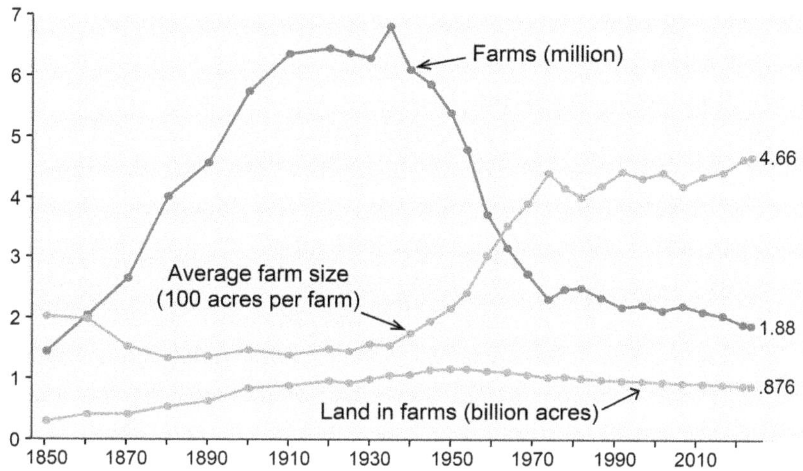

Figure 2.1 Farms, land in farms, and average acres per farm, 1850–2024.

Source: USDA, Economic Research Service using data from USDA, National Agricultural Statistics Service, Censuses of Agriculture (through 2022) and *Farms and Land in Farms: 2024 Summary* (February 2025).

increased in size and productivity (see Figure 2.1; Lacy, 2025). Throughout the 1970s, farming and the industries that supported agriculture were booming, making it the most profitable decade in U.S. agriculture history (Tevis, 2022).

This prosperity came to an abrupt halt by the end of the decade. A surge in farm expansion and production was made possible by taking on substantial debt, something that was encouraged by the federal government. When an influx of foreign grain and a spike in borrowing costs during the 1979 recession caused prices to plummet, farmers were unable to make payments on their debt, triggering the Farm Crisis of the 1980s. In the South, changes in agriculture meant Black farmers lost land ownership and the power that came with it (Holloway, 2021). Black farmers suffered disproportionately, losing their land at a rate 10 times that of White farmers (Davidson, 1996). The farm crisis devastated small towns, leading to the closure of vital local businesses, many of which never returned, and increased rates of alcohol abuse, depression, domestic violence, and suicide (Tevis, 2022). The outcome of the crisis would be both profound and long-standing as corporate ownership replaced family farms and local land ownership (Davidson, 1996).

The 1980s marked a shift toward manufacturing and service-sector jobs in rural communities (McGranahan, 2003). The intention was to create a pathway to the middle class through rural manufacturing growth (Summers & Clemente, 1976; Warren, 2014). Manufacturing jobs provided nonfarm employment options for people with high school diplomas, offering higher wages and benefits than other available jobs (Green, 2020; Green & Sanchez, 2007). However, rural economic conditions varied, and jobs that enabled a middle-class standard of living disappeared in some places (Lyson & Falk, 1993; Warren, 2014). Local leaders shifted their strategy to attract jobs, focusing on attracting low-skilled, low-wage industries. The approach was based on the belief that these jobs would boost income and create opportunities for poor residents with lower education and skill levels (Green, 2020). The reliance on low-wage jobs from outside, private-sector companies to boost local economic conditions did not contribute to the quality of life as intended. In *Broken Heartland*, Davidson (1996) describes how the reopening of a meatpacking plant in Columbus Junction, Iowa in 1985 brought the promise of jobs and hopes for a revitalized community. Two years earlier, the plant had closed resulting in the loss of hundreds of jobs.

> The plant meant jobs and jobs meant paychecks – steady money for a change, money that would circulate up and down Main Street like an ocean wave washing into an estuary. From the workers to the grocery stores, and from there to the barber shops, cafes, pharmacy, appliance and clothing stores. Taxes paid by the new homeowners would improve city services, which had dwindled during hard times. The local school would benefit from revenue, too. There were new textbooks to buy, sports programs to reinstate, computers to add. The children of Columbus Junction would have a shot at a brighter future. (p. 126)

Like many small towns at the time, the anticipated benefits from new jobs in Columbus Junction did not fully materialize. Although the town saw increased jobs and some new businesses, retail sales declined. The community faced an influx of poor newcomers seeking employment, leading to a housing shortage, rising homelessness, and increased pressure on social services. Rather than lifting rural communities and people, focusing on bringing low-wage, low-skill jobs left communities in a weakened position. It resulted in a greater divide between rural and urban economies, with higher-paying, higher-skill professional jobs locating in urban areas and lower-wage, lower-skill jobs disproportionately locating in rural areas (McGranahan, 2003). The geographic difference in opportunity prompted a brain drain as young adults left rural communities for higher-paying jobs in the city.

Many small towns were in a weakened position when the next economic shift, brought on by foreign competition, occurred in the late 1980s. Cheaper land and labor and an ongoing push for globalization since the Reagan era led to more foreign competition and the loss of manufacturing jobs overseas (Buttel, 2003). In the end, rural communities that had long relied on low-wage labor as a development strategy could not compete with low-wage workers in a global market (Falk & Lyson, 1988). Across many small towns, family-owned businesses with a long history of supporting local communities transformed into publicly traded corporations. Jobs that once provided steady incomes for generations disappeared as factories closed. Work moved overseas, where people earned just a fraction of what local workers once did. At the same time, families and entire rural communities struggled to adjust. What was once a source of pride and stability became a reminder of how globalization could reshape economies and whole communities (Flora et al., 2016). While urban, suburban, and rural areas have all been affected by economic restructuring over the last several decades, rural communities have taken the most significant economic hit (Smith & Tickamyer, 2011).

1990s to the Present: Globalization, the Internet, and New Era of Capitalism

Globalization, the internationalization of markets, and the rise of communication technologies in the late 1990s resulted in rapid advancements (Albrecht, 2007). Small towns were now competing in the global market, which was disastrous for single-industry towns such as textile producers in Georgia. After spending decades attracting low-paying industries, community leaders realized that seeking these jobs had led them down the wrong path. The course correction toward high-quality jobs proved difficult after decades of reliance on low levels of human capital (Flora et al., 2016).

The Great Recession had a particularly harsh impact on rural communities and its effects still linger. Job losses from 2008 to 2010 were lower in rural areas than in urban areas, possibly due to pre-existing high unemployment levels, yet economic recovery took much longer (Mattingly et al., 2011). Although there were regional variations, employment did not reach pre-recession levels in nonmetropolitan areas until 2015, and some rural areas had not yet recovered when COVID-19 arrived in 2020 (Rodden, 2024). Global demand for agricultural products moderated some of the impact of the Great Recession on rural areas while manufacturing jobs, especially those related to the housing sector, were a casualty (Flora et al., 2016). Public-sector jobs, an essential source of rural employment, have been the leading source of long-term job losses and a significant factor in the slow recovery (Rodden, 2024). In the wake of the Great Recession, men, young adults, people with lower educational attainment, and single parents have faced the highest unemployment rates in rural areas (Mattingly et al., 2011).

Rural economies are changing. In many communities, low-skilled manufacturing jobs have been replaced by growth in low-paying, service-sector jobs (Albrecht, 2014; Flora et al., 2016). Though service-sector jobs can include higher-paying jobs, the growth of these jobs has been difficult in rural areas due to the slow addition of broadband (Green, 2020). The Internet serves the same function as railroads and highways did in previous generations, making broadband a vital infrastructure in the information society. Like the slow expansion of electricity into rural areas a century ago, rural access to high-speed Internet has lagged behind urban areas. The inability to respond to technological changes has resulted in a spiral of disadvantage for many small towns. As revenues decline, some communities have decreased spending on education and infrastructure while at the same time offering incentives and subsidies to attract low-wage employers (Green et al., 2002). Attracting low-paying industries has been costly, leaving residents with depressed wages, underfunded school systems, limited access to higher education, and rising poverty (Flora et al., 2016). Young adults in disadvantaged communities disproportionately moved elsewhere for better opportunities, resulting in more significant demographic disadvantage and population loss through depopulation (Johnson & Lichter, 2019).

The story of America's small towns is one of boom-and-bust cycles and uneven patterns of growth and decline. Historically, geography and natural resources have played a role in uneven patterns of opportunity in rural communities, affecting economic development options, population growth or decline, access to services and amenities, and local housing needs. While the global economy has reduced the importance and connection between geography and natural resources in some ways, it has increased its significance in others (Albrecht, 2007). For example, as jobs in farming and natural resource extraction declined, leveraging natural resources for tourism and recreation has been an important source of economic growth for small towns. With the increase in remote work, small towns with amenities and aesthetic appeal are attracting residents who are no longer tethered to their employer's location (Vice News, 2021). At the same time, rural communities far outside urban areas with large swaths of flat land suitable for farming lose out if they lack aesthetic appeal, tourism attractions, or recreation amenities (Albrecht, 2007; McGranahan, 2003). A source of inexpensive land for manufacturing sites may be an asset, though likely limited to low-wage, low-skill jobs. When higher-skill manufacturing jobs move to rural areas, they are typically in communities near a larger city (McGranahan, 2003).

What Does the History of Rural America Have to Do with Housing?

Today, some small-town business districts are bustling as they did in the past. Others with vacant storefronts offer a reminder of the struggles of rural America. The present-day housing problems within these communities are rooted in a larger story, in which economic restructuring and government policies have overlooked the economic and housing needs of small towns and, at times, have implemented policies that adversely affected their fates. Economic restructuring has also left many communities reliant on the changing whims of the private sector in both thriving and struggling communities, resulting in the prosperity of a few at the expense of the community as a whole. This dynamic is evident among small towns in the West, where affluent newcomers have driven up housing costs, creating a housing crisis for the service-sector workers in the restaurants and shops that make these communities great places to visit and live. It is also evident in southern small towns experiencing persistent poverty, where housing affordability, substandard housing, and a lack of housing options for older adults are intractable problems.

There is hope. Small-town vitality and quality of life depend on finding or continuing a path forward. The path to a better quality of life for residents requires drawing on community strengths, building or leveraging amenity resources, sustainable economic development, and a sound infrastructure that includes a supply of housing that meets the needs of the community's present and future residents. Investing in housing infrastructure is essential for success. Housing supports Main Street and connects communities to resources and opportunities, just as other infrastructure elements like schools and roads do (Rosen et al., 2021). Housing is also central to economic development in small towns and essential to residents' quality of life and well-being (Anthony, 2023; Lubell, 2023; Basmajian & Rongerude, 2012; MacTavish et al., 2014; Ziebarth, 2015). In short, for rural communities to thrive, they need to consider housing. Small towns have the ingredients for a community-based approach to solving problems that will lead to a housing infrastructure that works for both economic development and quality of life. However, solving problems will require letting go of long-standing beliefs, a legacy of rural history in the U.S., and a willingness to embrace a new way of thinking about housing for the community.

References

Albrecht, D. E. (2007). Small town in global society. *Journal of Rural Social Sciences*, 22(1), 1–14. https://egrove.olemiss.edu/jrss/vol22/iss1/1

Albrecht, D. E. (2014). *Rethinking rural: Global community and economic development in the small town West*. Washington State University Press.

Anthony, J. (2023). Housing affordability and economic growth. *Housing Policy Debate*, 33(5), 1187–1205. https://doi.org/10.1080/10511482.2022.2065328.

Atack, J., Margo, R. A., & Rhode, P. W. (2022). Industrialization and urbanization in nineteenth century America. *Regional Science and Urban Economics*, 94, 103678. https://doi.org/10.1016/j.regsciurbeco.2021.103678

Basmajian, C., & Rongerude, J. (2012). Hiding in the shadow of Wagner-Steagall: Understanding rural public housing in the United States. *Journal of the American Planning Association*, 78(4), 406–414. https://doi.org/10.1080/01944363.2012.737980

Beale, C. (1993). Salient features of the demography of American agriculture. In D. L. Brown, D. Field, & J. J. Zuiches (Eds.), *The demography of rural life* (pp. 108–127). Northwest Regional Center for Rural Development.

Buttel, F. H. (2003). Continuities and disjunctures in the transformation of the U.S. agro-food system. In D. L. Brown, L. E. Swanson, & A. W. Barton (Eds.), *Challenges for rural America in the twenty-first century* (pp. 177–189). Pennsylvania State University Press.

Davidson, O. G. (1996). *Broken heartland: The rise of America's rural ghetto* (Expanded ed). University of Iowa Press.

Falk, W. W., & Lobao, L. M. (2003). Lessons from the past, challenges for the future. In D. L. Brown, L. E. Swanson, A. W. Barton, & Rural Sociological Society (Eds.), *Challenges for rural America in the twenty-first century* (pp. 152–165). Pennsylvania State University Press.

Falk, W. W., & Lyson, T. A. (Eds.). (1988). *High tech, low tech, no tech: Recent industrial and occupational change in the South*. State University of New York Press.

Flora, C. B., Flora, J. L., & Gasteyer, S. P. (2016). *Rural communities: Legacy and change* (Fifth edition). Westview Press.

Green, G. P. (2020). Deindustrialization of rural America: Economic restructuring and the rural ghetto. *Local Development & Society, 1*(1), 15–25. https://doi.org/10.1080/26883597.2020.1801331

Green, G. P., Haines, A., Dunn, A., & Sullivan, D. M. (2002). The role of local development organizations in rural America. *Rural Sociology, 67*(3), 394–415. https://doi.org/10.1111/j.1549-0831.2002.tb00110.x

Green, G. P., & Sanchez, L. (2007). Does manufacturing still matter? *Population Research and Policy Review, 26*(5–6), 529–551. https://doi.org/10.1007/s11113-007-9043-8

Hibbard, M., & Frank, K. (2021). The efficiency/community duality in the emergence of planning: Cases in rural regional development. *Journal of Planning History, 20*(1), 49–68. https://doi.org/10.1177/1538513220919960

Holloway, K. (2021). How thousands of Black farmers were forced off their land. *The Nation*, November 15/22. https://www.thenation.com/article/society/black-farmers-pigford-debt/

Jakle, J. A. (1999). America's small town/big city dialectic. *Journal of Cultural Geography, 18*(2), 1–27. https://doi.org/10.1080/08873639909478302

Johnson, K. M., & Lichter, D. T. (2019). Rural depopulation: Growth and decline processes over the past century. *Rural Sociology, 84*(1), 3–27. https://doi.org/10.1111/ruso.12266

Kley, A., & Paul, H. (2015). *Rural America*. Universitätsverlag Winter.

Lacy, K. (2025, March 12). *The number of U.S. farms continues slow decline* [Government]. US Department of Agriculture, Economic Research Service. https://www.ers.usda.gov/data-products/chart-gallery/chart-detail?chartId=58268

Lubell, J. (2023, August 14). Deconstructing the national housing dilemma. National Conference of State Legislatures Legislative Summit. https://documents.ncsl.org/wwwncsl/Summit/2023/Session-Resources/Lubell-Presentation-to-NCSL-Conference_2023_08_10-FINAL.pdf

Lyson, T. A., & Falk, W. W. (Eds.). (1993). *Forgotten places: Uneven development in rural America*. University Press of Kansas.

MacTavish, K., Ziebarth, A., & George, L. (2014). Housing in rural America. In C. Bailey, E. P. Ransom, & L. I. Jensen (Eds.), *Rural America in a globalizing world: Problems and prospects for the 2010s* (First edition). West Virginia University Press.

Mattingly, M., Smith, K., & Bean, J. (2011). *Unemployment in the Great Recession: Single parents and men hit hard* (No. 35; Issues Brief). Carsey School of Public Policy, University of New Hampshire. https://doi.org/10.34051/p/2020.144

McGranahan, D. A. (2003). How people make a living in rural America. In D. L. Brown, L. E. Swanson, & A. W. Barton (Eds.), *Challenges for rural America in the twenty-first century* (pp. 135–151). Pennsylvania State University Press.

Rodden, J. (2024). The Great Recession and the public sector in rural America. *Journal of Economic Geography*, 24(3), 441–458. https://doi.org/10.1093/jeg/lbad015

Rosen, K. T., Bank, D., Hall, M., Reed, S., & Goldman, C. (2021). *Housing is critical infrastructure: Social and economic benefits of building more housing*. Rosen Consulting Group. https://www.nar.realtor/sites/default/files/documents/Housing-is-Critical-Infrastructure-Social-and-Economic-Benefits-of-Building-More-Housing-6-15-2021.pdf

Smith, K. E., & Tickamyer, A. R. (2011). Introduction. In K. E. Smith & A. R. Tickamyer (Eds.), *Economic restructuring and family well-being in rural America* (pp. 1–21). Pennsylvania State University Press.

Summers, G. F., & Clemente, F. (1976). Industrial development, income distribution, and public policy. *Rural Sociology*, *41*(2), 248–266.

Tevis, C. (2022). The 1980s farm crisis: A boots-on-the-ground retrospective. *Agricultural History*, 96(4), 580–593. https://doi.org/10.1215/00021482-10009811

Tönnies, F. (1988). *Community & society*. Transaction Books.

Vice News. (2021, September 3). *This town was paradise, Then everyone started working from home*. https://www.youtube.com/watch?v=WhElNHGN9KY

Warren, W. J. (2014). Beyond the rust belt: The neglected history of the rural Midwest's industrialization after World War II. In J. L. Anderson (Ed.), *The rural Midwest since World War II* (pp. 72–102). Cornell University Press, NIU Press. https://www.jstor.org/stable/10.7591/j.ctvw1d4sf.9

Ziebarth, A. (2015). Renting in rural America. *Family and Consumer Sciences Research Journal*, 44(1), 88–104. https://doi.org/10.1111/fcsr.12121

Ziebarth, A., & Tigges, L. (2003). Earning a living and building a life: Income-generating and income-saving strategies of rural Wisconsin families. In W. W. Falk, M. D. Schulman, & A. R. Tickamyer (Eds.), *Communities of work: Rural restructuring in local and global contexts* (pp. 316–338). Ohio University Press.

3

WHY RURAL AND SMALL TOWNS ENTRUST HOUSING TO THE PRIVATE MARKET

The traditions and beliefs carried forward from rural America's history, combined with federal policies that fail to meet present-day realities, have left a lasting mark on how local leaders think about and respond to housing. Despite economic and demographic shifts that have transformed rural communities, the social identity of American small towns has persisted. Small towns are still considered to be places that are neighborly, have a sense of community spirit and pride, where everybody knows everybody, people are family-oriented and help one another (Hummon, 1990; Skobba, 2002). These small-town attributes suggest that community leaders should prioritize the well-being of residents. However, when housing issues emerge that compromise residents' or the economic health of the town, community leaders are unlikely to spring into action. Though positive social characteristics figure prominently in the small-town narrative, a different set of underlying values guides decision-making. Rooted in early American

DOI: 10.4324/9781003520450-3

values and beliefs, the markers of civic virtue—property ownership, personal responsibility, and economic opportunity—have long shaped small-town decision-making (Mattson, 1997). Understanding and responding to a community's housing needs falls outside this scope. Even if decision-makers sought a larger role in housing, they would find little federal policy support to enable it. As a result, local governments have kept their housing decisions small in scope—confined to setting the stage for private-sector development (Wiley, 2025).

Housing challenges in rural and urban places have become more alike than different over the past several decades, yet the federal policies and programs to address these challenges remain separate. Urban housing policies are guided by the U.S. Department of Housing and Urban Development (HUD), an agency focused exclusively on housing and community development. Rural housing initiatives, on the other hand, are integrated into broader development strategies of the U.S. Department of Agriculture (USDA) to enhance the economy and quality of life in rural America. The location of rural housing policy within USDA exhibits an outmoded association between rurality and agriculture (Basmajian & Rongerude, 2012). Consequently, rural housing has developed along a separate trajectory, with distinct policy objectives and institutional structures that place housing within the context of an agrarian lifestyle rather than within a coordinated national housing policy approach that considers housing needs for communities across the U.S. (Belden, 2019).

The case for separate policies and programs is that the USDA can offer (1) valuable insights and expertise regarding rural communities through its locally based offices and (2) its programs are specifically designed to meet the unique needs of these communities (Jones & McCarty, 2022). Funding and capacity deficits persist despite this specialized expertise and understanding of rural communities. Rural housing programs remain consistently underfunded and understaffed (Housing Assistance Council, 2023). The separation has translated into limited funding among a complex web of programs for rural communities, some that put them in direct competition with urban areas. Rural communities often lack the capacity to garner funding for programs offered through HUD, such as HOME and CDBG, which provide much-needed resources to address small-town housing and neighborhood issues, though the programs are primarily designed for urban communities.

Figure 3.1 Vacant house.

Photo credit: Authors.

The separation of rural and urban housing policies was intended to improve rural housing programs; it has instead resulted in a piecemeal approach while often obscuring rural housing issues (Basmajian & Rongerude, 2012). The placement of housing within an agricultural context has created a cloak of invisibility around rural housing issues. This cloak has shielded these programs from the stigma, public debates, and controversies surrounding federal rental assistance programs (Basmajian & Rongerude, 2012). Remaining unseen means rural housing challenges often come into focus only when they coincide with urban issues, such as during the Great Depression, the foreclosure crisis, and the current housing shortage and affordability crisis. For rural residents, the differential treatment is yet another example of their communities failing to receive a fair share of government funding, programs, and resources, further reinforcing a lack of trust in government to solve rural issues. With mindsets of government mistrust and strong views about private property, beliefs that government should stay out of private property issues remain entrenched (Jacobs, 2011). The result is a lack of local government involvement in housing issues. The problem of housing the community is deferred to somebody else—usually private-sector developers and landlords.

The Rural Perspective and Mindsets: Rooted in the Past, a Barrier in the Present

Rural residents share a perspective based on a common set of norms and beliefs, often unspoken, that shape how individuals and groups interact with one another. This perspective is rooted in a rural identity that includes an attachment to place and a connection with others who share the experiences and values of life in rural communities (Diamond, 2023). The rural perspective, however, is more than an identification or attachment to rural places. It also conveys how rural residents perceive power, values, lifestyle, and resources (Cramer, 2016). The rural perspective is a distinct culture with a core set of beliefs (Gabehart, 2023). We call these core beliefs *rural mindsets*. Rural mindsets are generated through shared experiences and are understood by rural residents regardless of where they live in the U.S. (Diamond, 2023; Sanchez & Vargas, 2016). Mindsets are a collection of shared mental models (Cabrera & Cabrera, 2022). Mental models are personal beliefs, values, and assumptions that guide our actions by shaping our perceptions, influencing how we interpret experiences and assess strategies (Bosch et al., 2019). Mental models are important because they shape what people consider possible, probable, and preferable. By examining six key mindsets, summarized in Table 3.1, we can better understand how deep-rooted beliefs impact housing decisions and development within rural communities. While many of these mindsets are embedded in broader U.S. culture, they figure prominently in how small-town Americans view each other and their communities.

Six Small-Town Mindsets That Influence Housing

Small-town mindsets influence local decision-making about housing. These mindsets might subtly appear in conversations about what, or for whom, housing is and is not needed. Whether implicitly or explicitly stated, small-town mindsets serve as powerful and guiding values that can impede local housing strategies. We examine the relationship between small-town mindsets and housing decision-making by focusing on these six key beliefs rooted in the rural perspective.

Mindset #1: People in small towns care for and are connected to family, neighbors, and community. One of the most common beliefs is that small towns have close social relationships. As discussed in Chapter 2, small towns have a cultural identity that is differentiated from large cities. The distinction between

Table 3.1 Small-Town Mindsets and Housing Implications

Small-Town Mindsets	*Housing Implications*
Close and caring social relationships	Ability to leverage social relationships and institutions to work together to solve housing problems May overlook people with weaker social connections
Single-family detached homeownership as the ideal	Other types of housing may not be considered Desire to limit rental housing in the community
Emphasis on independence and self-reliance	Entrepreneurial spirit is an asset when working on housing solutions Reluctance to consider solutions that involve the government or seek assistance from organizations or peer communities
Anyone can achieve material success through hard work and motivation	A lack of interest in housing solutions designed to meet the needs of a wide range of residents, especially those who face the greatest housing challenges in the community
A lack of trust and confidence in government to solve significant issues	Reluctance to include local government elected leaders and staff who are instrumental in community housing teams May undermine funding efforts that bring new housing or improve aging and substandard housing
The private market can do it better	Disinterest in the community housing approach and proactive housing problem-solving A housing inventory inadequate for current and future residents

rural and urban places includes a set of attributes based on social interactions and community life. This mindset includes a place-based identity, yet it is also deeply embedded in the worldview of rural and small-town residents (Cramer, 2016).

In the book, *Small-Town America: Finding Community, Shaping the Future*, Wuthnow (2013) writes:

> The town has an identity as a community. Its meanings are inscribed in particular places and the tangible aspects of these places – the

> park, school building, and stores on Main Street. The town's identity is reinforced in festivals and ball games, small acts of kindness, recovering from disaster, and the stories that are repeated about these events, and by the local cultural leaders who keep the stories alive.
> (p. 3)

In our case study research with Georgia Initiative for Community Housing participants, aspects of this mindset were reflected in the comments of community leaders, who described their towns as charming places offering a sense of community, where people get along, participate, and take pride in the community. One leader captured this dynamic of place and people, describing his small town as a community-oriented place where the downtown served as the collective front porch. Our research often included descriptions of small towns as friendly places where everybody knows everybody, and people actively participate in community events. I (Kim) found the same descriptions when conducting research on small-town identities in Minnesota nearly 25 years ago (Skobba, 2002).

The social characteristics attributed to small towns can serve as strengths when implementing a community housing approach. However, this mindset can also lead to complacency. As we will see in the other core mindsets, social relationships and the proverbial helping hand may not include *everyone* in the community.

Mindset #2: Land and property ownership, accomplished through single-family detached homeownership, as the small town ideal. Property ownership figures prominently in the history of rural America and continues to be a significant rural value (Flora et al., 2016; Jackson-Smith & Petrzelka, 2014). While property ownership began with land, typically farmland, today this cultural value is more likely to be achieved through single-family homeownership. While single-family, detached housing is the norm in the U.S., representing about 60% of all homes nationwide, this structure type is even more predominant in rural America, representing over 72% of all homes (Housing Assistance Council, 2023). Single-family detached housing has long been viewed as the most appropriate housing for families with children and the staple of stable neighborhoods (Wegmann, 2020). As homeowners age, the cost and responsibility of maintaining these homes can become untenable.

Small towns in the U.S. have aging populations with a prevalence of one- and two-person households and higher than average rates of poverty, suggesting a need for a diversity of housing types and options (AARP, 2019; Housing Assistance Council, 2023; Schroeder et al., 2021). The focus on single-family homeownership results in a lack of attention to the housing needs of rural renters (MacTavish et al., 2014). The emphasis on single-family homeownership also precludes consideration of other forms of housing that residents may need, leading to a critical absence of options along the rural housing continuum (Nash et al., 2011). This absence includes housing appropriate for young adults starting independent lives and older adults hoping to stay in the community as they age.

Mindset #3: The importance of independence and self-reliance. Self-reliance and a strong individualistic ethos—present since the earliest days of the country—are core values among rural people and places (Flora et al., 2016; Gimpel & Karnes, 2006). These values are linked to the origins of rural communities as economically independent places based on traditional economic activities. These values are an essential part of the rural perspective (Jackson-Smith, 2003). As we will see later in this chapter, it is a mindset that has shaped federal housing policy for rural communities. Closely tied to these values is the identity of rural and small-town residents as hard-working, self-sufficient people with preferences for self-employment and property ownership (Gimpel & Karnes, 2006). Gimpel and Kairnes note that while most rural entrepreneurs differ from CEOs in corporate America, they may feel a greater kinship with them compared to urban laborers who are beholden to their employees. Values of independence stand in contrast to perceptions of urban places and people, who are reliant on and receive more than their fair share of resources (Cramer, 2016).

Values of self-reliance and independence are evidenced in the desire for little or no government regulation (Gimpel & Karnes, 2006). It is a value that includes avoiding assistance from the government or outsiders (Diamond, 2023; White et al., 2003). Taken together, these values result in an approach to housing that favors the private market. It is an insular approach rather than a collaborative one. Addressing housing problems requires building local capacity by leveraging resources, ideas, and information from people and organizations outside of the community. Going it alone makes it more challenging to make any changes to the community's housing, let alone implementing the variety of changes needed in most small towns.

Mindset #4: Hard work leads to material success. The economic individualism in the previous mindset is linked to the belief that hard work leads to material success. The hard work/material success mindset is part of the long-standing cultural belief that America is the land of opportunity and that anyone can achieve material success with motivation and perseverance, regardless of their background (Lichter & Crowley, 2002; Quart, 2023). A corollary of this belief is that poverty and low wages result from personal shortcomings rather than labor market conditions or economic policies (Flora et al., 2016; Sherman, 2014). This mindset is reflected in the commonly held notion of bootstrapping. Bootstrapping is the belief that you can get ahead on your own resources, right attitude, and hard work. It is a belief held by most Americans regardless of where they live or their political affiliation (Rooks, 2012). Even so, bootstrapping is also an impossible myth—both unattainable and unrealistic. The impossibility of going it alone is reflected in the origins of "pull yourself up by your bootstraps," which was originally a joke used to mock the absurdity of the idea. Take a closer look at the origins of most "self-made" wealthy entrepreneurs and you will find they received help from family, investors, and often, government subsidies (Davies, 2023). As Quart (2023), author of the book *Bootstrapped* points out, everyone needs resources and support to succeed in life. People need support from their community through infrastructure, education, the collective tax base, and support from family and friends.

The hard work/material success mindset persists in small towns despite the history of low-wage business attraction as a core economic development strategy, poverty rates among young and old alike, underfunded schools, and widening achievement gaps. This belief determines who is and is not worthy of help in rural communities. This mindset is also reflected in attitudes about welfare and government programs serving low-income households (Gimpel & Karnes, 2006). The belief that people can move up the socio-economic ladder through sheer will and hard work undermines the progress of rural communities by restricting access to the resources and support that people need to prosper. Notions of the unworthy poor lead to the denial of basic needs, such as affordable housing, which undermines community vitality. This belief also results in a lack of interest in solutions designed to meet the needs of a wide range of residents. Ultimately, the hard work/material success mindset limits community potential and throttles one of the best attributes of small towns—the ability to leverage relationships and social institutions to work together to solve problems.

Mindset #5: A well-earned lack of trust in government to solve problems. Trust and confidence in the government to solve significant issues is at an all-time low, especially among rural residents. Past experiences, which have left rural residents feeling that government does more harm than good in their communities, likely contribute to this mindset. While some policies and programs have drastically improved the circumstances and lives of rural families, others have either neglected rural communities or have been detrimental to their prosperity. If you talk with small-town leaders with once-thriving textile industries, NAFTA will inevitably come up, even among young city staff who were not yet born when it was enacted. These varied, and often unfavorable experiences have left rural residents weary of government intervention (Gabehart, 2023).

The lack of trust among rural residents includes a perception that their communities have been left behind, receiving less than their share of beneficial government funding, programs, and resources (Kirk, 2025). The history of federal funding and policies for rural housing and community development supports this sentiment. Add declining economic conditions and inadequate public services, and it should come as no surprise that rural and small-town residents lack or have a flagging faith in government. Distrust of government often extends to public employees, who are thought to embody the values and priorities of people from urban places, even when they live in small towns (Cramer, 2016). In contrast to the prototypical rural resident who is independent, hardworking, and cares about family and community, public employees are thought to be lazy, overpaid, and wasteful of tax dollars (Cramer, 2016). Thus, the mental model of small towns is that they are not big government, nor are they supportive of it (Wuthnow, 2013). This mindset can undermine efforts to bring much-needed new housing or funds to improve aging and substandard housing. Ties between local leaders and state and federal government staff can play a vital role when beginning to address housing using a community-based approach and is something to revisit in a later chapter.

Mindset #6: The private market can do it better. Embraced by both political parties in the U.S. over the past several decades, belief in private market solutions is not limited to rural places and people. However, it is a particularly entrenched belief in small towns (Gimpel & Karnes, 2006). The "private market can do it better" mindset is linked to other rural mindsets. A logical contrast to a floundering and wasteful government is the belief in an effective and efficient private market. The private market mindset is also linked to the economic individualism associated with independence and self-reliance, which favors support of private business and entrepreneurship, and values widespread property ownership (Gimpel & Karnes, 2006). It is a mindset connected to the belief that hard work leads to material success.

Faith in the private market to deliver jobs, goods, and services prevails despite resulting in uneven and underdevelopment with some rural communities experiencing prosperity while others are declining (Warner, 2003). This confidence has led to an elevation of private-sector interests over the public good and support of the social safety net (Lobao, 2014). Numerous examples in Chapter 2 illustrate how the private sector has undermined the quality of life in rural America and has often resulted in the prosperity of a few at the expense of many.

Before turning to the problems of leaving housing to the private sector, we want to reiterate that we are not in any manner against private-sector housing. The players in private-sector housing, including developers, homebuilders, multifamily property owners, and landlords, provide an important and necessary function in housing Americans. They are essential partners in the community housing approach. In changing the way in which decisions about housing are made, private developers can become proactive partners rather than a counterpoint to housing discussions.

The Costs of a Hands-Off Approach to Housing

The hands-off approach to housing comes with costs. The approach results in an extremely limited range of housing types, which affects both the "haves" and "have-nots." Housing problems linger, becoming apparent when the unmet needs within the community surface as the population increases or declines, residents age, or young adults decide to move back to their hometown. As a result, even individuals who have achieved some material success may not find a supply of housing ready and waiting for them. The changing economic conditions in rural communities make leaving the responsibility of housing to private market development a risky endeavor. In good economic conditions, the housing industry is present but noticeably absent when the communities experience economic downturns or distressed conditions. In short, not engaging in a housing conversation leaves communities with a housing inventory inadequate for current and future residents.

Stewart,[1] Georgia is a small town a little too far for a reasonable commute to Atlanta but about 30 minutes from a city of 100,000. A local government staff member described how the city had approached housing in the past: *The city's position was to completely leave that (housing) to the private market and just say yes or no as far as it fit with what was allowed. And really was to not engage in that conversation.* When Stewart entered the Georgia Initiative for Community Housing, the quaint downtown was seeing some signs of revitalization. The community was home to a few manufacturing companies but was lacking a range of retail businesses. This former mill town also had some troubling statistics. Over half of the children in the community were living below the poverty level. Nearly a quarter of the residents over age 25 had less than a high school diploma (U.S. Census Bureau, 2024). About half of the households were considered low-income (U.S. Department of Housing and Urban Development, 2024). The majority of the households in Stewart, Georgia, rented their homes, which included a substantial amount of substandard housing. An astounding percentage of low-income renter households experienced housing cost burden. Despite these significant affordability problems, the general feeling in the community was that there was already too much low-income rental housing in the city. With its proximity to larger cities and land available for future housing and business development, Stewart was on the precipice of growth, with no plan in place for new housing development.

Legacy Problems in Your Community

The "no engagement" approach to housing embraced in Stewart is common among small-town leaders. A combination of factors has contributed to this approach. Economic restructuring and inadequate federal and state housing policies have left many rural communities with depleted financial and human capital. Small towns are also hindered by shared cultural beliefs that can impede local housing decision-making. The lack of community-based, proactive planning in small towns leaves behind a host of legacy problems - outdated zoning ordinances, aging and deteriorating housing, extended-stay hotels serving as rental housing, and a lack of housing options. We refer to these issues as legacy problems because they are often the result of the collection of mindsets discussed in this chapter. The housing in small towns is influenced by mindsets of self-reliance and independence, preferences for private property ownership, beliefs about who is and is not worthy of help, lack of trust in government, and misplaced confidence that the private market does things better—all of which contribute to legacy problems. These legacy problems can create enduring barriers for local leaders seeking to improve their community's housing.

Before closing this chapter, we thought it might be helpful to provide a brief list of common legacy issues that may be hindering your community. Recognizing these problems can help you begin to move beyond past hurdles.

- Your community needs more capacity to address housing problems, but leaders are unwilling to seek outside advice or assistance.
- The predominant housing option available is single-family housing and residents and community leaders quickly shut down discussions about any other housing type.
- Maintaining or increasing homeownership is always the focus, even when there is a demonstrable need for more rental housing in the community.
- Community members state that there is too much affordable housing, even though the housing supply is limited, or housing cost-burdened households are common.
- Many jobs in the community pay a low wage, but housing within a worker's budget is unavailable and actively resisted.
- Elected officials treat some words as curse words (affordable, apartments, density, low-income, project) and drop them from their vocabulary when talking about housing.
- Economic development is bringing jobs, but its impact on the need for more or different housing is rarely, if ever, discussed at the same time.

Up to this point, we have framed small-town mindsets as hindering housing in the community. However, small towns can leverage these mindsets to benefit a community housing approach. We have observed how small-town mindsets go from a detriment to an asset when housing problems become too big to ignore, and someone in the community recognizes there is an opportunity for action. To get to that point, community leaders need to recognize the problems that have been hiding in plain sight. The housing, demographic, and economic problems that are both visible and measurable but remain overlooked.

Note

1 Stewart is a pseudonym. See Appendix for more information.

References

AARP. (2019). *Making room: Housing for a changing America*. AARP and National Building Museum. https://www.aarp.org/livable-communities/housing/info-2018/making-room-housing-for-a-changing-america.html

Basmajian, C., & Rongerude, J. (2012). Hiding in the shadow of Wagner-Steagall: Understanding rural public housing in the United States. *Journal of the American Planning Association*, 78(4), 406–414. https://doi.org/10.1080/01944363.2012.737980

Belden, J. (2019). Why doesn't rural housing get any respect? *Shelterforce*. https://shelterforce.org/2019/06/19/why-doesnt-rural-housing-get-any-respect/

Bosch, O., Nguyen, N., Van Thanh, N., Malik, F., & Malic, C. (2019). *Systems thinking for everyone: The journey from theory to making an impact*. Malik Institute/Malik International AG.

Cabrera, D., & Cabrera, L. (2022). DSRP theory: A primer. *Systems*, 10(2), 26. https://doi.org/10.3390/systems10020026

Cramer, K. J. (2016). *The politics of resentment: Rural consciousness in Wisconsin and the rise of Scott Walker*. University of Chicago Press.

Davies, D. M. (2023, March 12). How harmful is the myth of bootstrapping? *Texas Public Radio*. https://www.tpr.org/podcast/the-source/2023-03-12/how-harmful-is-the-myth-of-bootstrapping

Diamond, E. P. (2023). Understanding rural identities and environmental policy attitudes in America. *Perspectives on Politics*, 21(2), 502–518. https://doi.org/10.1017/S1537592721002231

Flora, C. B., Flora, J. L., & Gasteyer, S. P. (2016). *Rural communities: Legacy and change* (Fifth edition). Westview Press.

Gabehart, K. M. (2023). Rural society, democratic exclusion, and the cultural divide: Moving towards a research agenda of the study of ruralness. *Public Integrity*, 25(5), 484–493. https://doi.org/10.1080/10999922.2022.2061132

Gimpel, J. G., & Karnes, K. A. (2006). The rural side of the urban-rural gap. *PS: Political Science & Politics*, 39(03), 467–472. https://www.jstor.org/stable/20451785

Housing Assistance Council. (2023). *Taking stock*. Housing Assistance Council. https://takingstockrural.org/taking-stock/

Hummon, D. M. (1990). *Commonplaces: Community ideology and identity in American culture*. State University of New York Press.

Jackson-Smith, D. B. (2003). Transforming rural America: The challenges of land use change in the twenty-first century. In D. L. Brown, L. E. Swanson, A. W. Barton, &

Rural Sociological Society (Eds.), *Challenges for rural America in the twenty-first century* (pp. 305–316). Pennsylvania State University Press.
Jackson-Smith, D., & Petrzelka, P. (2014). Land ownership in American agriculture. In C. Bailey, E. P. Ransom, L. I. Jensen, & Rural Sociological Society (Eds.), *Rural America in a globalizing world: Problems and prospects for the 2010s* (First edition, pp. 51–68). West Virginia University Press.
Jacobs, H. M. (2011). Rarely managing growth: The under-utilization of land use policy approaches. In D. W. Marcouiller, M. B. Lapping, & O. J. Furuseth (Eds.), *Rural housing, exurbanization, and amenity-driven development: Contrasting the "haves" and the "have nots"* (pp. 259–280). Ashgate.
Jones, K., & McCarty, M. (2022). *USDA rural housing programs: An overview* (No. R47044). Congressional Research Service. https://crsreports.congress.gov/product/pdf/R/R47044
Kirk, J. R. G. (2025). Landscape of distrust: Political trust across America's urban-rural divide. *American Politics Research*, 53(1), 28–35. https://doi.org/10.1177/1532673X241273220
Lichter, D. T., & Crowley, M. L. (2002). Poverty in America: Beyond welfare reform. *Population Bulletin*, 57(2), 1–36. https://www.prb.org/wp-content/uploads/2021/02/06052002_57.2PovertyInAmerica.pdf
Lobao, L. M. (2014). Economic change, structural forces, and rural America: Shifting fortunes across communities. In C. Bailey, L. Jensen, E. Ransom, & Rural Sociological Society (Eds.), *Rural America in a globalizing world: Problems and prospects for the 2010s* (First edition, pp. 543–555). West Virginia University Press.
MacTavish, K., Ziebarth, A., & George, L. (2014). Housing in rural America. In C. Bailey, E. P. Ransom, & L. I. Jensen (Eds.), *Rural America in a globalizing world: Problems and prospects for the 2010s* (First edition, pp. 677– 692). West Virginia University Press.
Mattson, G. A. (1997). Redefining the American small town: Community governance. *Journal of Rural Studies*, 13(1), 121–130. https://doi.org/10.1016/S0743-0167(96)00039-3
Nash, B., Folts, W. E., Muir, K. B., Peacock, J., & Jones, K. (2011). Elderly populations and the rural urban continuum. In D. W. Marcouiller, M. B. Lapping, & O. J. Furuseth (Eds.), *Rural housing, exurbanization, and amenity-driven development: Contrasting the "haves" and the "have nots"* (pp. 75–91). Ashgate.
Quart, A. (2023). *Bootstrapped: Liberating ourselves from the American dream* (First edition). HarperCollins Publishers.
Rooks, N. M. (2012, September 7). The myth of bootstrapping. *Time*. https://ideas.time.com/2012/09/07/the-myth-of-bootstrapping/
Sanchez, G. R., & Vargas, E. D. (2016). Taking a closer look at group identity: The link between theory and measurement of group consciousness and linked fate. *Political Research Quarterly*, 69(1), 160–174. https://doi.org/10.1177/1065912915624571
Schroeder, J., Henning-Smith, C., & Tuttle, M. (2021). *Demographics and disability status of adults living alone in rural areas* [Policy Brief]. University of Minnesota Rural Health Research Center. https://rhrc.umn.edu/wp-content/uploads/2021/09/UMN-Policy-Brief_Demographics-and-Disability-Status-of-Rural-Adults-Living-Alone_3.23.21_508.pdf
Sherman, J. (2014). Rural poverty: The Great Recession, rising unemployment, and the underutilized safety net. In C. Bailey, L. Jensen, & E. Ransom (Eds.), *Rural America*

in a globalizing world: Problems and prospects for the 2010s (First edition, pp. 523–542). West Virginia University Press.

Skobba, K. R. (2002). *The role of location and ideology in small town housing policy decisions* [Master of Arts Thesis]. University of Minnesota.

U.S. Census Bureau. (2024). *American Community Survey 2019–2023 (5-Year estimates)* [Dataset].

U.S. Department of Housing and Urban Development. (2024). *Comprehensive Housing Affordability Strategy (CHAS) 2017–2021 data* [Dataset].

Warner, M. E. (2003). Competition, cooperation, and local governance. In D. L. Brown, L. E. Swanson, & A. W. Barton (Eds.), *Challenges for rural America in the twenty-first century* (pp. 252–261). Pennsylvania State University Press.

Wegmann, J. (2020). Death to single-family zoning…and new life to the missing middle. *Journal of the American Planning Association*, *86*(1), 113–119. https://doi.org/10.1080/01944363.2019.1651217

White, J., Tickamyer, A. R., Henderson, D. A., & Tadlock, B. (2003). Does welfare to work work? Rural employers comment. In W. W. Falk (Ed.), *Communities of work: Rural restructuring in local and global contexts* (pp. 240–265). Ohio University Center for International Studies.

Wiley, R. J. (2025). *Policymakers' perceptions about providing affordable housing in rural Georgia*. https://www.proquest.com/openview/f2023cc07cbfe271e6fa355d2be4e76c/1?pq-origsite=gscholar&cbl=18750&diss=y

Wuthnow, R. (2013). *Small-town America*. Princeton University Press.

4

PROBLEMS WAITING TO BE SEEN

SMALL-TOWN HOUSING REALITIES

At some point, housing issues reach a level that is hard to ignore. The U.S. housing shortage and affordability crisis have reached this critical point over the past several years. When problems reach peak levels, they seem like they came out of nowhere. A housing crisis can happen suddenly when a hurricane, tornado, or wildfire moves through, leaving the community with urgent housing needs. More often, housing challenges unfold gradually, hiding in plain sight. The current housing shortage, rising rents, and increasing home prices in the U.S. have recently garnered significant attention in local and national news. Yet, the factors contributing to these challenges have been developing over decades. The signs were there long before the crisis became a daily news story. A similar phenomenon happens in small towns. As decisions are postponed, housing problems accumulate, waiting to be noticed.

DOI: 10.4324/9781003520450-4

Common Housing Challenges in Small Towns and Rural Areas

Housing Issues Associated with Population Growth and Decline

Over the past 20 years, small towns and rural areas have lost population, while communities in and on the edge of urban areas (exurban) have had significant population gains (Table 4.1). While rural small towns have experienced a net loss, there is variation among these communities. Driven by recreation and tourism-based economies and natural amenities, some rural areas are experiencing growth. At the same time, more geographically isolated places face significant population losses (Lichter & Johnson, 2025). This population loss is accompanied by economic stagnation, higher poverty rates, and brain drain as younger adults move to places with greater opportunity (Housing Assistance Council, 2023b; Lichter & Johnson, 2025).

Whether gaining or losing populations, these changes affect rural communities and their housing needs. Growth stimulates the demand for additional housing, while population decline decreases housing demand. Community housing needs within these two scenarios are more nuanced. The housing needed in communities with increasing demand is shaped by the community demographic characteristics, including household income, size, and the age distribution of householders.

In small towns losing population, housing conditions tend to decline over time as longtime residents age, and homes lose value, becoming substandard and eventually vacant (Flora et al., 2016; Salamon & Tornatore, 1994; Wang, 2018). Despite poorer housing conditions, households experience housing cost burdens and housing insecurity due to high poverty

Table 4.1 Population Change 2000–2020

Year	*Small Town and Rural*	*Suburban and Exurban*	*Urban*	*U.S.*
2000	61,382,344	128,934,408	91,105,154	281,421,906
2020	60,260,519	154,897,478	116,291,275	331,449,281
Change (%)	−1.9	20.1	27.6	17.8

Source: Housing Assistance Council (2023a).

rates and low household incomes (Dumont, 2018; Fitchen, 1992; MacTavish et al., 2014; Ward, 2016). The economic realities of these communities make it difficult to attract outside help. The private market is neither interested in nor equipped to address housing needs, and federal resources are not designed to improve housing conditions in rural areas (Dumont, 2018).

In places with increasing populations, typically small towns outside of urban or amenity-rich areas, the private market is active, improving existing and developing new housing. These communities attract more affluent professionals and retirees, driving up the cost of land values and housing (Lawson & Smith, 2023; MacTavish et al., 2014; Marcouiller et al., 2016). Housing development of higher cost primary and vacation for more affluent homebuyers is common (Hamilton et al., 2008; MacTavish et al., 2014; Marcouiller et al., 2016). Residents earning low and moderate incomes, particularly renters, may find that the affordable housing options are either occupied or do not exist in the community (MacTavish et al., 2014; Ward, 2016). Mobile home parks provide an essential source of affordable housing in these communities. Yet, rising land values incentivize park owners to sell, putting this housing at risk (Salamon & MacTavish, 2017). Additionally, new mobile home parks are unlikely to be developed in exurban and amenity-rich areas because of zoning ordinances and a lack of interest from municipalities (Salamon & MacTavish, 2017).

Community leaders do not need to look at Census data to become aware of these changes. Visible, everyday signs of growth or decline serve as a reminder. Signs of population decline show up in vacant houses, shuttered stores, and fewer kids in the school district. Growth shows up in construction activity, a bustling main street, and people participating in community life—in churches, local businesses, and schools.

Existing Housing Types Do Not Match Household Demographics

Another common challenge facing rural and small towns is the lack of housing options needed to meet the needs of residents of different income levels, ages, and household sizes. Most housing in small towns and rural areas is single-family detached housing, followed by manufactured housing (Figure 4.1).

While most households in small towns are homeowners, a little over a quarter of rural households rent their homes. Many of these renters live

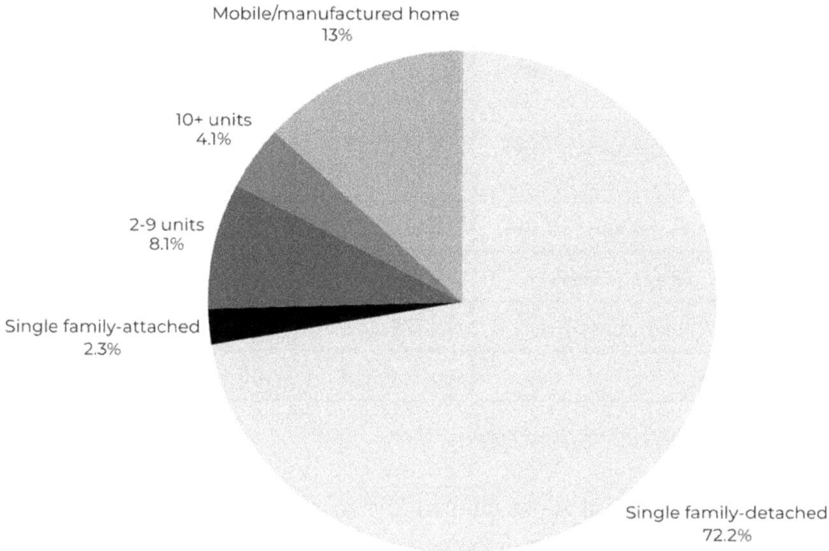

Figure 4.1 Structure types in small towns and rural areas.

Source: Authors, using data from the Housing Assistance Council (2023a).

in single-family homes or manufactured housing (Housing Assistance Council, 2023b). The predominance of single-family detached housing may no longer meet the needs of many rural households. About two-thirds of rural households in the U.S. have only one or two people. Households without children are expected to increase over the coming decades (AARP, 2019). Yet, smaller-scale, multifamily housing with two to nine units, often called "missing middle" housing, well-suited for smaller households, is uncommon, comprising about 8% of housing units in rural and small towns. Multifamily housing with 10 or more units, a standard rental option, is about 4% of the rural housing stock. This lack of housing diversity is a feature of small towns. It exists regardless of population dynamics and geographic location.

The lack of housing options leaves gaps for many current and future residents—young adults, low- and moderate-income workforce, aging residents, and single parents. Few options are available for the workforce when new jobs come to town. Young adults moving into the community or returning may need or prefer an apartment rather than take on the responsibility of a single-family home. Older adults looking to downsize will find

Table 4.2 Age of Population in Small Towns and Rural Areas

Age Group	#	*Small Town/ Rural (%)*	U.S. (%)
Children and adolescents (0–19 years old)	14,752,272	24.48	24.80
Early/mid-working age (20–44)	17,435,732	28.93	32.94
Prime working age (45–64)	15,894,147	26.38	25.43
Retirement/older adults (65+)	12,178,368	20.21	16.83
Total	60,260,519	100	100

Source: Housing Assistance Council (2023a).

few options, making it more challenging to age in place. Like population change, the lack of housing options is visible to community leaders. Drive around town, and it is easy to see that most housing is best suited for families with children. The lack of housing options might also surface in conversations with residents, business owners, and real estate professionals who experience the challenges of the community's housing mismatch in their daily lives (Table 4.2).

Housing Is Less Affordable and in Worse Condition

Like the U.S. overall, housing costs in small towns and rural areas are misaligned with household incomes. Housing affordability problems affect both renters and homeowners. Close to one-fifth of homeowners in small towns and rural areas are housing cost burdened, meaning they pay more than 30% of their income on housing costs. The situation is more dire for rural renters. About 45% of the small-town and rural renters are housing cost burdened, meaning they pay more than 30% of their income on housing costs. Over 20% are paying over half of their household income on housing costs (Figure 4.2). With the supply of subsidized rental housing declining in rural areas, low-income renters are increasingly at risk of housing cost burden (Scally et al., 2018). When households spend too much on their housing, they may not have enough left to cover other expenses such as food, transportation, and medical expenses.

Housing in small towns and rural areas is often older and needs significant maintenance, rehabilitation, or demolition. While housing quality has

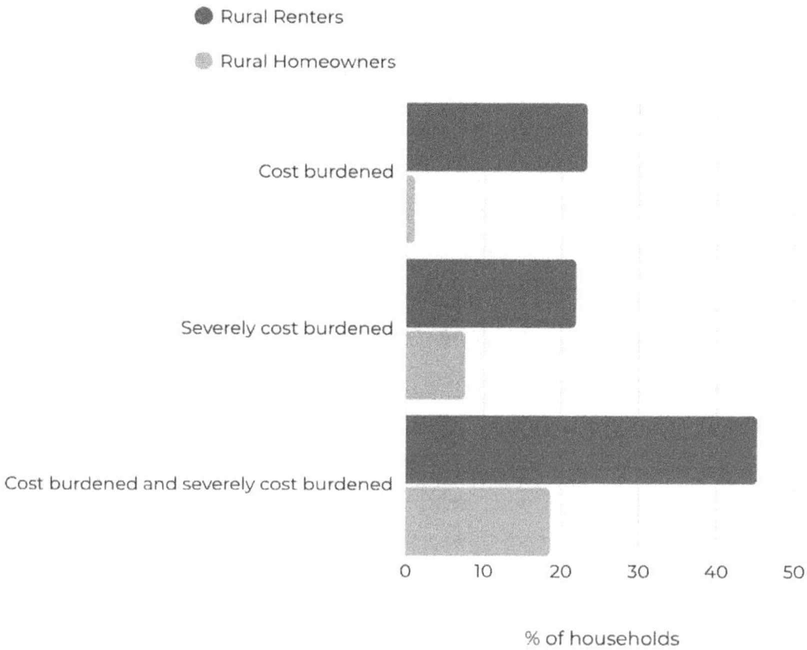

Figure 4.2 Housing cost burden among small-town renters and homeowners.
Source: Housing Assistance Council (2023a, 2023b).

improved in America's rural towns, substandard housing is still a lingering challenge, with over 5% of rural homes classified as inadequate (Housing Assistance Council, 2023b). This statistic is likely an underestimate of the problem in some regions. In our statewide survey in Georgia, a majority of rural community leaders identified dilapidated and vacant housing as a challenge (Skobba et al., 2020). Data on rural communities often show high housing vacancy rates, which may give the appearance of an adequate supply of available housing. However, in some areas, vacant homes may indicate that the housing is dilapidated and unhabitable.

Common Small Town Types and Their Housing Problem Signals

Every small town is unique, yet there are commonalities related to population growth or decline, community attributes, local economies, and housing conditions. We have organized rural and small towns into five types based on these and other characteristics. Categorizing rural and small towns can be a helpful shorthand for recognizing common elements and challenges long before action is taken to tackle housing problems. Our typology draws on previous conceptualizations by Albrecht (2007), Hamilton et al. (2008), and Salamon (2010). We have added rural tribal and native communities as a separate community type. Below we describe each community type and characteristics of people, location, economic conditions, and how they affect community housing needs and challenges.

Thriving Hometowns

Thriving Hometowns are rural small towns with aesthetically pleasing physical attributes—bodies of water, picturesque landscapes, historic buildings, often located near a major highway or interstate (Salamon, 2010). Their economic base is relatively strong and does not rely on the rural agricultural and resource-dependent industries of the past (Albrecht, 2007). Small town character, attractive features, and location, and local economic conditions set the stage for population growth and service-sector businesses (Albrecht, 2007). The newer side of Thriving Hometowns has suburban housing developments and chain restaurants. The older part of town includes a mix of smaller homes, historically significant homes, and a main street with independent shops and restaurants (Salamon, 2010).

Thriving Hometowns experience various housing challenges, including a lack of affordable housing for the local workforce and rental housing options for younger and older residents. Developers respond to growth pressures by building suburban developments with larger single-family homes that serve the higher-income new residents. Longtime residents, particularly young adults, may be priced out of the homeownership market. If rental housing and small-unit townhouse or condo developments exist, they are marketed for affluent households. Housing options for less affluent residents are overlooked. Rising housing costs combined with limited housing options lead to a mismatch between local wages and housing costs, creating a housing crisis for the community's lower-wage workforce. With few affordable homeownership options, even moderate-income families may struggle to find housing that meets their needs, prompting them to move out of the community. Lower-income residents may face housing instability and homelessness, though these problems may remain invisible outside of school districts, churches, and nonprofit organizations.

Amenity Gateway Communities

Amenity Gateway communities are located near areas rich in natural beauty (forests, lakes, mountains, rivers, and other scenic landscapes) and amenities, which boost their local economies through recreation and tourism or offer the potential for economic growth (Bergstrom & Harrington, 2018; Hamilton et al., 2008; Stoker et al., 2021). Communities with established local economies based on tourism and recreation have a vibrant business district with retail, restaurants, and services. These communities are more remote than Thriving Hometowns.

Amenity Gateways attract affluent residents and retirees, creating income inequalities between newcomers, longtime residents, and the local workforce (Stoker et al., 2021). New housing development in Amenity Gateway communities caters to affluent residents, second-home owners, and investment properties for vacation and short-term rental housing. Housing costs increase for renters and homeowners, creating affordability and access issues for less affluent residents. The service-industry workers needed to support the businesses essential to the local economy will have few housing options, placing them at risk of overcrowding, living in poor-quality housing, and homelessness. Local business owners may be the first to draw attention to the problem when the lack of housing affects their ability to hire and retain employees.

Steady Legacy Towns

Steady Legacy Towns lack aesthetic amenities but have relatively stable populations and local economies. Without adequate amenities and located at an inconvenient distance from large cities, these communities do not attract growth from more affluent populations and the service-sector businesses that follow them (Albrecht, 2007). Communities in this category may have experienced past economic hardships when major employers closed, resulting in a loss of population (Albrecht, 2007; Duncan, 2014). Steady Legacy Towns have maintained or achieved economic stability over time, often through a mix of strategies that include agriculture and resource-based jobs, manufacturing, public-sector employment, and innovative, nonfarm businesses (Albrecht, 2007; Duncan, 2014; Salamon, 2010; Wojan & Parker, 2017). The lower cost of living and availability of jobs may attract some new residents, who offset population losses.

Housing challenges in Steady Legacy Towns include an aging housing stock needing repair, a lack of available housing options, and some affordability pressures. While a modest amount of new housing construction activity may exist, pockets of substandard and dilapidated housing persist in the community. These communities have an insufficient supply of subsidized rental housing for low-income households, lack quality rental housing options and homeownership opportunities for moderate-income families, and have few appropriate options for older adults.

Withering Outposts

Withering Outposts are remote, lack amenities and jobs, and have declining populations. These communities are among the most disadvantaged, often due to geographic isolation and long-term dependence on traditional agricultural and manufacturing employment, which has left them without a viable economic base (Albrecht, 2007). Withering Outposts have high poverty rates, historic underinvestment, and deteriorating infrastructure and housing conditions (Duncan, 2014; Hamilton et al., 2008). In the middle of the U.S., Withering Outposts are likely to have many adults aged 65 and older. In contrast, eastern and western states have higher proportions of younger residents (Cromartie, 2018).

With declining populations, these communities have numerous housing challenges. The existing housing in the community is in poor condition yet remains unaffordable due to prevalent poverty. Housing is often substandard or dilapidated and difficult to finance for new construction or renovation due to a lack of market value. Population decline means there is little incentive for private developers to invest, leading to a cycle of underinvestment and decline.

Tribal and Native Communities

Tribal and Native Communities have characteristics that set them apart from other small-town types, even though they may share similarities. Among American Indian and Alaskan Native populations in the U.S., over half live in rural and small towns, with the majority living on or near their tribal homelands (Dewees & Marks, 2017). While these communities are not monolithic, they share a history of colonialism and oppression that has shaped the trajectories of their people and communities, which warrants a separate category in the small-town typology. Individual tribal and native communities can and do have characteristics that fit within the small town types described above. Like rural communities in general, tribal and native communities in the U.S. have historically relied on economic activities focused on natural resources, manufacturing, utilities, services, and public-sector employment (Klingbeil et al., 2023). Though they share similar economic development strategies, tribal and native communities differ significantly in governance, land management, jurisdiction, cultural identity, and general beliefs from U.S. rural communities (Klingbeil et al., 2023).

The housing challenges in tribal and native communities, like all rural and small towns, are influenced by the degree of geographic remoteness, household income, employment opportunities, and economic investment. Native households have lower median household incomes compared to the U.S., and about one-third live in poverty (National Low Income Housing Coalition, 2024). Households living on tribal lands are significantly more likely to live in overcrowded and poor housing (National Low Income Housing Coalition, 2024). While most rural Native households on tribal lands own their home (about 70%), communities often lack affordable rental properties due to limited private rental investment. Lack of infrastructure is a considerable barrier.

In the next chapter, we provide an in-depth look at what happens once a community faces a significant housing problem and why getting to this point is often the culmination of years or decades of relegating local housing solely to the private sector. Although these problems are often visible, reported by community members, and documented in the data, they remain unaddressed. At some point, these problems (and others) become too big to ignore, and someone in the community recognizes a need for action. We call this pivotal point the Eureka Moment. The spark may happen with growth from more affluent residents, pressures from new and expanding industries bringing an influx of workers, or the failure to attract much-needed economic development. Regardless of circumstance, rural and small towns have the ingredients to bring about change in community housing. They just need the recipe.

References

AARP. (2019). *Making room: Housing for a changing America*. AARP and National Building Museum. https://www.aarp.org/livable-communities/housing/info-2018/making-room-housing-for-a-changing-america.html

Albrecht, D. E. (2007). Small town in global society. *Journal of Rural Social Sciences, 22*(1), 1–14. https://egrove.olemiss.edu/jrss/vol22/iss1/1

Bergstrom, R. D., & Harrington, L. M. B. (2018). Understanding agents of change in amenity gateways of the Greater Yellowstone region. *Community Development, 49*(2), 145–160. https://doi.org/10.1080/15575330.2017.1416648

Cromartie, J. (2018). Rural aging occurs in different places for very different reasons [Government]. *Economic Research Service*. https://www.usda.gov/about-usda/news/blog/rural-aging-occurs-different-places-very-different-reasons

Dewees, S., & Marks, B. (2017). *Twice invisible: Understanding rural Native America* (No. 2; Research Note). First Nations Development Institute.

Dumont, A. M. (2018). Rural affordable rental housing: Quantifying need, reviewing recent federal support, and assessing the use of Low Income Housing Tax Credits in rural areas. *Finance and Economics Discussion Series, 2018.0*(77). https://doi.org/10.17016/feds.2018.077

Duncan, C. M. (2014). *Worlds apart: Poverty and politics in rural America* (Second edition). Yale University Press.

Fitchen, J. M. (1992). On the edge of homelessness: Rural poverty and housing insecurity. *Rural Sociology, 57*(2), 173–193. https://doi.org/10.1111/j.1549-0831.1992.tb00462.x

Flora, C. B., Flora, J. L., & Gasteyer, S. P. (2016). *Rural communities: Legacy and change* (Fifth edition). Westview Press.

Hamilton, L., Hamilton, L., Duncan, C., & Colocousis, C. (2008). *Place matters: Challenges and opportunities in four rural Americas* (No. 4:1). The Carsey Institute. https://doi.org/10.34051/p/2020.41

Housing Assistance Council. (2023a). *Tabulations of U.S. Census Bureau's American Community Survey (ACS) five-year estimates* [Dataset]. Rural Data Central.

Housing Assistance Council. (2023b). *Taking stock*. Housing Assistance Council. https://takingstockrural.org/taking-stock/

Klingbeil, K., Adler, C., Hermans, A., Maher, H., Pindus, N. M., & Whitehead, D. (2023). *Community economic development in Indian country: Market research report*. CDFI Fund, Big Water Consulting, and Urban Institute. https://www.cdfifund.gov/system/files/2023-10/CDFI_NMT_NI_Market_Research_Report_Final.pdf

Lawson, M., & Smith, K. (2023). *The amenity trap: How high-amenity communities can avoid being loved to death*. https://headwaterseconomics.org/outdoor-recreation/amenity-trap/

Lichter, D. T., & Johnson, K. M. (2025). Depopulation, deaths, diversity, and deprivation: The 4Ds of rural population change. *RSF: The Russell Sage Foundation Journal of the Social Sciences, 11*(2), 88–114. https://doi.org/10.7758/RSF.2025.11.2.05

MacTavish, K., Ziebarth, A., & George, L. (2014). Housing in rural America. In C. Bailey, E. P. Ransom, & L. I. Jensen (Eds.), *Rural America in a globalizing world: Problems and prospects for the 2010s* (First edition, pp. 677–692). West Virginia University Press.

Marcouiller, D., Lapping, M., & Furuseth, O. J. (Eds.). (2016). *Rural housing, exurbanization, and amenity-driven development*. Routledge. https://doi.org/10.4324/9781315607160

National Low Income Housing Coalition. (2024). *Native American housing*. https://nlihc.org/explore-issues/policy-priorities/native-american-housing

Salamon, S. (2010). *Newcomers to old towns: Suburbanization of the heartland*. University of Chicago Press.

Salamon, S., & MacTavish, K. (2017). *Singlewide: Chasing the American dream in a rural trailer park*. Cornell University Press. https://ebookcentral.proquest.com/lib/ugalib/detail.action?docID=4982966

Salamon, S., & Tornatore, J. B. (1994). Territory contested through property in a Midwestern post-agricultural community. *Rural Sociology, 59*(4), 636–654. https://doi.org/10.1111/j.1549-0831.1994.tb00552.x

Scally, C. P., Gilbert, B., Hedman, C., Gold, A., & Posey, L. (2018). *Rental housing for a 21st century rural America*. Urban Institute. https://www.urban.org/research/publication/rental-housing-21st-century-rural-america

Skobba, K., Osinubi, A., & Tinsley, K. L. (2020). What about rural blight? Housing and neighborhood conditions in southeastern small towns. *Rural Sociology, 85*(1), 85–110. https://search.ebscohost.com/login.aspx?direct=true&AuthType=ip,shib&db=edsbl&AN=vdc.100103548943.0x000001&site=eds-live&custid=uga1

Stoker, P., Rumore, D., Romaniello, L., & Levine, Z. (2021). Planning and development challenges in Western gateway communities. *Journal of the American Planning Association, 87*(1), 21–33. https://doi.org/10.1080/01944363.2020.1791728

Wang, H. (2018). Home improvement investment in rural America. In D. E. Albrecht, S. Loveridge, S. Goetz, & R. Welborn (Eds.), *Rural housing and economic development* (pp. 247–268). Routledge. https://www.taylorfrancis.com/reader/read-online/489d925c-4036-4824-b764-2321aeeb2572/book/epub?context=ubx

Ward, S. (2016). Chronic poverty, community decline, and amenity-rich growth in rural America. In D. Marcouiller, M. Lapping, & O. J. Furuseth (Eds.), *Rural housing, exurbanization, and amenity-driven development: Contrasting the "haves" and the "have nots."* (pp. 157–173). Ashgate.

Wojan, T., & Parker, T. (2017). *Innovation in the rural nonfarm economy: Its effect on job and earnings growth, 2010–2014* (Economic Research Report No. 238). Economic Research Service, U.S. Department of Agriculture.

5

THE EUREKA MOMENT

OUR COMMUNITY HAS A HOUSING PROBLEM

In Chapter 1, we introduced Greenfield,[1] a small town in Georgia with 6,000 residents, facing growth from an auto components manufacturer bringing 2,500 new jobs. Greenfield's existing housing problems had been overlooked until the announcement of the impending arrival of this company, the most recent in a string of economic development wins. This latest announcement opened community leaders' eyes to the town's housing challenges. Leaders in Greenfield had reached a pivotal moment.

When housing concerns peak, community leaders often experience a motivational spark, realizing they have a housing problem. We call this spark the *Eureka Moment*. The problem may become known, as it did in Greenfield, when the pressures from new industries bring an influx of workers to the community's doorstep. Sometimes, housing needs become apparent when new, more affluent residents arrive, creating affordability and availability problems for longtime residents and workers. The Eureka Moment may unfold slowly, as a creeping awareness that the housing stock is impeding

DOI: 10.4324/9781003520450-5

much-needed economic development. These situations and many others are real problems. Problems that we know from experience take a long time to address. A Eureka Moment is routinely defined using the words "triumphant" and "discovery." While recognizing your community's housing problems may not feel triumphant, discovering that the local housing market is not working for the community is a momentous occasion. The Eureka Moment is the vital first step to addressing housing challenges.

How Community Leaders Arrive at the Eureka Moment

Communities applying to the Georgia Initiative for Community Housing (GICH) program have experienced the Eureka Moment. An analysis of program application materials over 10 years suggests that rural and small-town leaders act when housing problems become hard to ignore. Sometimes, recognition starts when a person of influence within the community encounters a housing issue firsthand. One community's Eureka Moment occurred when a pastor encountered untenable living conditions while helping a parishioner. Outraged after observing a collapsed ceiling and rats in the parishioner's rented home, the pastor contacted a code enforcement officer, who promptly condemned the apartment, leaving the parishioner without a place to live. While assisting in his parishioner's housing search, the pastor learned there were very few adequate, affordable rental options in the community. He began advocating for more affordable housing in the community, finding a group of people who shared his concerns. This discovery that a community lacks adequate and affordable housing is described, albeit less dramatically, in many applications to the GICH program. The catalyst for awareness comes in different forms—pressures from growth or large-scale economic development activity, the inability to replace or fix housing damaged from a natural disaster, or the recognition that housing is key to turning around a stagnant economy and declining population.

Eureka Moments have three key ingredients: (1) the recognition that the community has a housing problem; (2) the belief that it will affect the community; and (3) the desire to act. These three ingredients align with research on problem-solving and action. Situational theory of problem solving (STOPS) provides a framework that links problem recognition to action (Grunig, 1997; Kim & Grunig, 2011). The STOPS model includes four key elements (Kim & Grunig, 2011):

- Problem-recognition—People observe a problem or situation, reflect on it, and realize that action is needed.
- Relevance—Problem-solving behavior occurs when people feel connected to the problem and consider it important.
- Constraints—The actual or perceived barriers to solving the problem. Constraints can prevent problem-solving action if they are perceived to be insurmountable.
- Communication action—Gathering, evaluating, and sharing information about the problem.

The framework was initially developed as a way of understanding the role of information in economic development (Grunig, 1969). The STOPS model has since been used as a model for predicting and explaining problem-solving and action on a range of societal issues (Chon & Chung, 2024; Lamm et al., 2018; Tao et al., 2024).

Eureka Moment as a Problem-Solving Process

From Problem-Solving to Action

We see the STOPS process when talking with community leaders who reach out to us for advice about housing problems in their community. We see problem recognition and relevance as community leaders describe the housing challenges in their community, how they have intensified, and how they are now negatively affecting the community in some way. We see the constraints and communication action at play as these leaders recognize the size and shape of their community's housing challenges and the desire to learn as much as possible about how to begin addressing these issues.

To see what the STOPS model looks like in practice, we examine a conversation with Susan (*pseudonym), an executive director for a nonprofit social service organization serving a rural county in Georgia. Susan reached out for advice about the growing homelessness problem in the county. The issue of homelessness, present for several years but largely hidden, was now readily apparent, garnering the attention of community leaders from the public school system, social service organizations, and concerned residents who wanted to do something about it. The community leaders and residents had achieved *problem recognition*—they had observed the problem and decided that action was needed. Susan went on to highlight the problem's *relevance* to community leaders. The issue was affecting many organizations and people in the community, including nonprofit organizations and schools that saw greater demand for services. The problem inspired a sense of urgency. A group of community leaders decided to start working on solutions. Noting one of the *constraints*, Susan described how her organization provided much-needed services to people experiencing homelessness but lacked the resources and capacity to tackle this pressing housing issue. She initiated our conversation as part of the group's information-gathering process. The group had entered the *communication action* stage; they were seeking more information about the issue of homelessness in rural communities and wanted to understand strategies they could use to begin solving the problem.

The conversation with Susan highlights the importance of the Eureka Moment in addressing community housing problems. As the saying goes, the first step in solving a problem is recognizing that there is one. The Eureka Moment goes beyond problem recognition. It also includes a consideration of barriers and a belief that the housing problem is crucial enough to seek information actively and purposefully. When Susan reached out for information, she had reached the Eureka Moment. She recognized a problem, and it was relevant enough to inspire her to seek out and share information about solutions.

An Unfolding Process

The term Eureka Moment implies a flash of insight. In reality, it is a process that unfolds over months. Figure 5.1 illustrates the Eureka Moment process for housing, adapted from Kim and Grunig's (2011) STOPS model. The third step, problem-solving barriers, can be a stopping point on the path to adopting a community housing approach if the barriers are perceived to be too big to overcome. The fourth step, the desire to take action, represents the transition from the Eureka Moment to the community housing approach.

To provide another example of how the Eureka Moment unfolds as a problem-solving process, we use a case example from Windspur,[2] a small town in southwestern Kansas. For leaders in this community, a meeting in 2007 was the start of their Eureka Moment. A group of community stakeholders, including bankers, developers, real estate agents, and local

Figure 5.1 The Eureka Moment in housing problem-solving.

Source: Authors, based on Kim and Grunig (2011).

employers, pointed out several housing problems in the city. Rental housing was substandard and overpriced; homes for sale were too expensive, and financing was scarce. Windspur had achieved problem recognition—it had a housing problem and a small group of stakeholders who felt the problem was significant. They also recognized they could overcome capacity constraints if the city and private sector worked together to address the problem. Over the next year, community leaders moved from problem recognition to information gathering. They hired a consultant group to conduct a community housing assessment, which initiated collective action to address the community's housing challenges, and a community housing approach is still in place today.

Waiting for the Eureka Moment

If you are a community leader or concerned citizen reading this book, you may have personally reached the Eureka Moment about your community's housing. This book may be your first step in seeking information. You may be gathering information while waiting for others to join you in understanding the urgency and importance of your community's housing problems. While the problem-solving framework in this chapter helps explain why the Eureka Moment is an essential first step in identifying solutions, it also provides insight into why housing problems go unrecognized or unaddressed despite recognition by people in the community.

We have studied, worked, and lived in small towns in different states and regions of the U.S. In our collective experience, we have yet to find housing nirvana—the community that provides ample, affordable, and appropriate housing across a continuum of options. All rural (and suburban and urban) communities in the U.S. have housing problems. Many communities, some of which are highlighted in this book, are actively working toward building a robust housing infrastructure. These communities all had housing problems that remained unrecognized and unaddressed at some point. Many more communities have substantial housing problems but have yet to experience or act on the Eureka Moment. As discussed in the previous chapters, a common reason for inaction is that rural and small-town leaders do not see housing as their responsibility. Instead, housing is considered a problem for the private market to solve. We have discussed how and why this approach ultimately leads to problems. So, why do some community leaders act on housing problems while others remain unconcerned or wait for housing problems to intensify? While the research on this question is slim, Kim and Grunig's (2011) STOPS model provides insights into why housing problems go unaddressed, even when community leaders have identified that a problem exists. Using the model, we have identified three barriers that impede community leaders from addressing housing problems: lack of awareness or disinterest in housing problems, community leaders not seeing housing problems as relevant or urgent, and constraints that limit problem-solving.

Lack of Awareness or Disinterest in Housing Problems

Problem-solving action requires that community leaders recognize that a problem exists. However, our research indicates many small-town decision-makers are reluctant to identify housing affordability and availability as problems, even when housing data for their community suggests otherwise (Osinubi et al., 2022). Affordable housing is not viewed as a need, even when a significant proportion of a community's lower-income households are facing housing cost burden. The need for more rental housing is overlooked even as rental vacancy levels are extremely low, suggesting a supply deficit. Decision-makers more readily acknowledge issues with dilapidated housing and housing with significant maintenance issues, suggesting that community leaders are more likely to identify visible problems (Skobba & Tinsley, 2019). And yet, visibility is no guarantee of problem recognition.

The lack of community leaders' recognition of housing availability and affordability as problems may stem from differences between demographic characteristics of community leaders, who are typically older and more affluent than residents overall. Differences in political dynamics and decision-making in small towns may also lead to a lack of awareness or acknowledgment of housing needs for low-income households. In small towns, decisions often depend heavily on the input and expertise of a limited group of influential individuals (Flora et al., 2016). In contrast, local governments in larger cities are more likely to engage in deliberative processes involving a wider array of participants, including various experts (Oliver, 2012). Housing quality problems, even when visible from a home's exterior, may remain out of sight and mind for community leaders due to segregated residential patterns in the U.S. (Diaz-Valenzuela et al., 2022). Image and small-town identity may also hinder the acknowledgment of significant problems. As we mentioned in Chapter 3, the mindset of small towns as places with community spirit and vitality, where everybody knows everybody and people look out for one another, may lead to complacency, especially when considering problems that affect the most disadvantaged residents.

The lack of awareness or interest in housing problems points to another critical aspect of the Eureka Moment—the influence of the person who recognizes the problem. There are people in every community who have a deep understanding of local housing problems because they live with the problems every day. Despite their experiences, knowledge of the problem remains isolated due to residents' lack of power and voice. The story of the pastor's experience seeing a community member's poor housing conditions highlights how influence matters in problem recognition.

Decision-Makers Do Not See Housing Issues as Important

Significant housing problems can remain unchanged in a community when issues are not considered important. This lack of concern creates a barrier to achieving the second crucial element in problem-solving—relevance. As with many societal challenges, people often do not think about housing problems unless they or someone they know is personally affected. Community leaders are more likely to remain passive when they have a weaker personal connection to the problem (Grunig, 1997). The relevance of housing problems is also linked to several of the mindsets identified earlier in this book. The emphasis is on property ownership, specifically single-family homeownership, which may lead to a perspective that devalues renter-related housing problems (MacTavish et al., 2014). The belief that hard work leads to material success, and the embrace of bootstrapping may lead decision-makers to consider the problems of lower-income residents as self-inflicted. Previous research suggests that local governments, particularly in small towns, are less responsive to disadvantaged community members (Schaffner et al., 2020). Add the belief that the private market is better at solving local problems, and it is not hard to see how housing fails to attract the attention of small-town decision-makers. If the problem lacks relevance, community leaders are unlikely to have the motivation to seek solutions.

Problem-Solving Constraints Are Insurmountable

Leaders who recognize housing problems exist and feel they are worth solving may stop seeking solutions if they encounter constraints perceived to be insurmountable. In his early work studying entrepreneurship and economic development, Grunig (1989) describes how significant constraints can impede problem-solving, stating: "People do not communicate about problems or issues about which they believe they can do little or about behaviors they do not believe they have the personal efficacy to execute (p. 212). If the initial information-seeking process yields constraints perceived to be unmanageable, community leaders are unlikely to get past the Eureka Moment. While community leaders may encounter various constraints, two in particular hinder progress—a perceived lack of public support and limited capacity to solve the problem.

A community housing approach to problem-solving is most successful when it includes a group of engaged stakeholders and a broad support base. However, the mindsets that create barriers to housing problem relevance may also make this approach unpopular, mainly when housing problems involve lower-income residents and housing options other than single-family homeownership. The smaller scale of rural communities means that elected officials, staff members, and other stakeholders interact more frequently with community members than in urban areas. Due to this proximity, community leaders are less likely to engage in problem-solving if housing issues are unpopular with residents (Trautman, 2016; Wuthnow, 2013). This potential constraint, however, may be diminishing as housing challenges become more widespread. An increasing percentage of Americans cite the rising cost of housing as a significant concern (DeSilver, 2024). Research suggests that local policies allowing for more homes, a wider variety of home types and sizes, and increased affordability, once met with resistance, are receiving support from many residents in rural, suburban, and urban areas (Horowitz & Kansal, 2024).

Addressing housing issues also requires local capacity to solve problems. While rural communities face many of the same problems and issues as their urban counterparts, the capacity to respond to concerns about housing quality, availability, and affordability is often scarce (Flora et al., 2016; Morton et al., 2004; Ziebarth et al., 2010). Having people in the community who can assess and analyze local housing needs, develop a housing plan, and form partnerships with the state and federal governments is essential to changing the local housing conditions. Having the ability to apply for funding from state and federal programs that support affordable housing for low-income households is also necessary (Landis & McClure, 2010). Navigating these programs is complicated and often requires local governments to strengthen their capacity to be competitive.

From Eureka Moment to the Community Housing Approach

The Eureka Moment is a pivotal point for community leaders. It is the moment of spark when housing problems are both evident and essential. The Eureka Moment is the start of problem-solving action, one that can lead from a private market to a community housing approach. It is also a point at which motivation for change can stall in the face of overwhelming constraints or the opposition of a few loud voices. Moving beyond the Eureka Moment requires letting go of long-standing mindsets, taking a few risks, having a desire to build capacity, and a lot of patience.

If you are reading this book because you have identified housing challenges in your community and want to begin addressing them, you are already engaged in problem-solving by seeking out information. We hope that you will not only finish this book but also continue gathering information about the housing problems in your community. Finding others who care about local housing issues is integral to the process. If you know of others who have experienced the Eureka Moment, begin sharing your information. Do you know of other communities in the area or state that have successfully tackled their housing issues? If so, reach out to them. Learning from different communities has been one of the most powerful tools in the GICH program. The remaining chapters in this book provide the blueprint for a community housing approach, including how to build a local team of stakeholders who are motivated to find solutions to the community's housing problems, gain public support, use data to understand the issue(s), and develop local capacity to implement solutions. Along the way, we provide tools and strategies to turn the initial motivational spark into the beginning of a process to proactively address housing deficits by introducing additional, diverse, or improved housing options.

We have spent time in this and previous chapters discussing things that have impeded progress in small towns. We wanted to end this chapter by highlighting the strengths that communities can leverage when they reach the Eureka Moment. In the Strong Towns blog titled "What's so Special About Small?" Durand-Wood (2024) uses the phrase "*we may not be big, but we're small*" to convey the nuanced strengths of small towns. The author notes that the small scale of towns saves time during community development. People know each other and are used to working together, which makes division of labor and consensus-building easier. In small towns, everyone can contribute to small, repeated changes. These minor improvements add up, generating an outsized impact in small places. Finally, unlike larger cities, small towns are nimble, operating like a kayak on a river—light, responsive, and able to change direction with a single paddle stroke, navigating currents and obstacles with agility unmatched by larger boats.

In the next chapter, you will see how this ability to pivot is a strength when shifting a community housing approach—an approach in which local leaders are proactive in creating housing that meets the needs of present and future residents.

Notes

1 Greenfield is a pseudonym. See Appendix for more information.

2 Windspur is a pseudonym. See Appendix for more information.

References

Chon, M.-G., & Chung, A. (2024). Driving climate action via government public relations: The role of government-citizen relationships and situational perceptions. *Journal of Public Relations Research*, 36(5), 407–425. https://doi.org/10.1080/1062726X.2024.2354177

DeSilver, D. (2024). A look at the state of affordable housing in the U.S. *Pew Research Center*. https://www.pewresearch.org/short-reads/2024/10/25/a-look-at-the-state-of-affordable-housing-in-the-us/

Diaz-Valenzuela, J., Holman, M., Zhang, Y., & Skobba, K. (2022). Local leaders' perceptions of housing access and segregation in their communities. *Family and Consumer Sciences Research Journal*, 50(4), 272–287. https://doi.org/10.1111/fcsr.12439

Durand-Wood, E. (2024). What's so special about small? *Strong Towns*. https://www.strongtowns.org/journal/2023/8/3/whats-so-special-about-small

Flora, C. B., Flora, J. L., & Gasteyer, S. P. (2016). *Rural communities: Legacy and change* (Fifth edition). Westview Press.

Grunig, J. E. (1969). Information and decision making in economic development. *Journalism Quarterly*, 46(3), 565–575. https://doi.org/10.1177/107769906904600315

Grunig, J. E. (1989). Publics, audiences and market segments: Models of receivers of campaign messages. In C. T. Salmon (Ed.), *Balancing social values and social change*,(pp. 199-228). Sage.

Grunig, J. E. (1997). A situational theory of publics: Conceptual history, recent challenges and new research. In Danny Moss, Toby MacManus, Dejan Verčič (Eds.), *Public relations research: An international perspective* (First edition, pp. 3–47). International Thomson Business Press.

Horowitz, A., & Kansal, T. (2024). Support for policies that promote more housing crosses geographic lines. *Pew Charitable Trust*. https://pew.org/3HGbp3q

Kim, J.-N., & Grunig, J. E. (2011). Problem solving and communicative action: A situational theory of problem solving. *Journal of Communication*, 61(1), 120–149. https://doi.org/10.1111/j.1460-2466.2010.01529.x

Lamm, A. J., Warner, L. A., Lundy, L. K., Bommidi, J. S., & Beattie, P. N. (2018). Informing water-saving communication in the United States using the situational theory of problem solving. *Landscape and Urban Planning*, 180, 217–222. https://doi.org/10.1016/j.landurbplan.2018.09.006

Landis, J. D., & McClure, K. (2010). Rethinking federal housing policy. *Journal of the American Planning Association*, 76(3), 319–348. https://doi.org/10.1080/01944363.2010.484793

MacTavish, K., Ziebarth, A., & George, L. (2014). Housing in rural America. In C. Bailey, E. P. Ransom, & L. I. Jensen (Eds.), *Rural America in a globalizing world: Problems and prospects for the 2010s* (First edition, pp. 677–692). West Virginia University Press.

Morton, L. W., Allen, B. L., & Li, T. (2004). Rural housing adequacy and civic structure. *Sociological Inquiry*, 74(4), 464–491. https://doi.org/10.1111/j.1475-682X.2004.00101.x

Oliver, J. E. (with Ha, S. E., & Callen, Z.). (2012). *Local elections and the politics of small-scale democracy* (First edition). Princeton University Press.

Osinubi, A., Skobba, K., Ziebarth, A., & Tinsley, K. (2022). Perceptions and affordable rental housing: A small-town perspective from Georgia. *Housing and Society*, 49(2), 187–208. https://doi.org/10.1080/08882746.2021.1940447

Schaffner, B. F., Rhodes, J. H., & La Raja, R. J. (2020). *Hometown inequality: Race, class, and representation in American local politics*. Cambridge University Press.
Skobba, K., & Tinsley, K. (2019). *Survey of rural small town housing in Georgia*. UGA Housing and Demographic Research Center.
Tao, W., Tian, S., Sunny Tsai, W.-H., & Seelig, M. I. (2024). The power of emotional appeal in motivating behaviors to mitigate climate change among Generation Z. *Journal of Nonprofit & Public Sector Marketing*, *36*(1), 37–64. https://doi.org/10.1080/10495142.2022.2133058
Trautman, R. R. (2016). Small-town policy makers. *Public Administration Review*, *76*(2), 221–224. https://doi.org/10.1111/puar.12526
Wuthnow, R. (2013). *Small-town America*. Princeton University Press.
Ziebarth, A., Prochaska-Cue, K., & Shrewsbury, B. (2010). Growth and locational impacts for housing in small communities. *Rural Sociology*, *62*(1), 111–125. https://doi.org/10.1111/j.1549-0831.1997.tb00647.x

6

THE PIVOT

A BLUEPRINT FOR CHANGE

Community leaders in Bellehaven[1] had cataloged their housing challenges. They had a full grasp of the impact their housing issues were having on the community. This relatively affluent small town of 5,000, known for its charming main street and historic architecture, had few housing options, some concerning housing quality issues, and a deficiency of housing affordable to the local workforce, which was hindering economic development opportunities. The community's dominant single-family, owner-occupied climate made it difficult for Bellehaven's small planning staff to approve multifamily and other forms of housing that would provide a greater range of options. Residents were not supportive of housing near them that would be affordable to people earning the $25,000–$60,000 salary common for jobs in the community. Bellehaven's community leaders and planning staff were ready to switch from discussing the problem to working on solutions. They recognized that providing housing for the community would require looking at housing differently.

DOI: 10.4324/9781003520450-6

The pivot to viewing housing challenges based on community needs and acknowledging the role of local government in making housing happen is an essential step toward a community housing approach. The community housing approach is proactive, locally led, and action-oriented. It draws on local social capital by bringing community leaders and stakeholders together. It uses data to identify housing needs within the community. It builds the capacity of local stakeholders to address the community's housing needs through the development of partnerships and networks. It is the opposite of deferring the responsibility of housing to the private market.

Core Components of the Community Housing Approach

The core components of the community housing approach include:

- Recognizing that housing problems exist within the community.
- Identifying a representative group of stakeholders, including local government staff and leaders, to serve on the community housing team.
- Building local political will and community buy-in to lay the groundwork for change.
- Collecting and analyzing community and neighborhood data.
- Gaining knowledge of funding sources, federal/state housing programs, and implementation strategies as leverage to address local housing issues.
- Developing an action-oriented work plan that includes measurable goals, potential resources, and is updated regularly.
- Cultivating a network of local partners, peer communities, nonprofit organizations, and state and federal housing agency representatives.

The community housing approach involves a chain of decisions and actions (Cook et al., 2009). Improvements in housing, whether bringing substandard housing up to code or adding new affordable rental or homeownership units, begin with engaging a local team of people (a community housing team) who are dedicated to understanding and addressing housing issues. The housing team identifies community housing needs, plans activities to address deficiencies, and locates financial resources to change the local housing supply. This process draws on social capital, as community leaders build a network of relationships and resources. Building the capacity of community members in this way contributes to the sustainability of community housing initiatives by strengthening residents' ability to carry out projects and planning efforts into the future (Kennedy, 2007). A process that involves both the development of housing and residents will result in an increased capacity of both, which generates the capacity to meet future housing needs.

Influences Shaping the Community Housing Approach

Community Development Principles and Social Capital Theory

If you have worked on community-based projects, the components of the community housing approach may look familiar. The approach uses the basic principles of community development often included in housing capacity-building and technical assistance programs. Fundamentally, community development is (1) a process that develops or enhances the capacity of local leaders to collaborate and (2) something that improves the community as a result of the action (Phillips & Pittman, 2015). Community development principles, guided by social capital theory, involve engaging stakeholders and building a network of relationships and resources to create positive change in the community. Social capital is the resource that comes from our investment in relationships (Brisson, 2009; Coleman, 1988; Putnam, 2001). A powerful resource woven into our relationships and networks, social capital opens doors to opportunities, enhances our ability to share ideas and information, and empowers us to take action, ultimately helping us achieve our goals (Häuberer, 2011; Ling & Dale, 2014). Leveraging these networks opens pathways, providing new connections with influential institutions that extend beyond local communities (Ling & Dale, 2014). Social capital plays a vital role in maximizing housing and economic development resources. The differences we see among communities often arise from varying levels of social capital. Engaging citizens in civic activities is fundamental for fostering economic growth (Putnam, 1993). Thriving communities are built on the ability of residents to collaboratively tackle local housing challenges (Morton et al., 2004).

Drawing on the expertise and time investment of local leaders, residents, and institutional resources is crucial in developing the community development capacity and action that leads to improvement (Phillips & Pittman, 2015). Community leaders, including elected officials, local government and nonprofit staff, and business owners, play a key role in the community housing approach. Their knowledge of the community, influence, and ability to mobilize resources are invaluable in addressing housing issues. They enhance community capacity through their individual skills to organizational strengths, leadership, networks, and are a community problem-solving resource (Chaskin, 2001).

Georgia Initiative for Community Housing and National League of Cities

The community housing approach originates in two related programs: (1) the Georgia Initiative for Community Housing and (2) a National League of Cities program called Strengthening Partnerships for Housing Opportunities. The Georgia Initiative for Community Housing is a statewide program spanning two decades, assisting over 100 communities. It began in 2004 as a follow-on to the state's participation in the National League of Cities program, which ran from 1998 to 2005. Both programs recognized that small cities, towns, and rural communities must build social, human, and political capital to create a multifaceted and sustained housing and community development program (Tinsley & Massey, 2009). The core components of the community housing approach stem from these two programs and have been expanded through our research and insights as practitioners.

Georgia Initiative for Community Housing

Since 2004, the Georgia Initiative for Community Housing has operated as a collaborative partnership between the University of Georgia's Center for Housing and Community Research in the College of Family and Consumer Sciences, Georgia Department of Community Affairs, Georgia Municipal Association, and Georgia Power. In a news article announcing the launch of the program, Jim Higdon, the executive director of the Georgia Municipal Association at the time, underscored the influence of the National League of Cities program. Higdon remarked,

> Housing is a major challenge facing many communities throughout Georgia, and one thing the National League of Cities program taught us is that city officials cannot solve it alone. It must be a collaborative approach that provides all key stakeholders an opportunity to identify

> the issues and develop comprehensive strategies for addressing them. That's what we hope to accomplish through this new initiative.
> (Mann, 2004)

The Georgia Initiative for Community Housing is a three-year program. The program typically admits five new communities annually through a competitive application process. While the program focuses on smaller communities, participants include a wide range of urban and rural communities. Each participating community forms a housing team that broadly represents the community, including city officials and staff, nonprofit groups, business owners, school district representatives, residents, and others interested in addressing local housing issues. Housing team members from all participating communities attend two conference-style retreats each year, which offer five elements: education on housing issues, programs, and tools, facilitated work time, peer learning, and networking. Each community-based housing team is assigned a facilitator, who works with the team to develop a work plan that outlines specific activities required to achieve identified objectives. During each retreat, housing teams have dedicated time in the agenda to discuss progress, update their work plan, and incorporate new plans based on information they have learned at the retreat. While local teams also meet outside of the retreat, this focused time working with a facilitator is an important aspect of the program.

During their time in the program, each community housing team typically follows a similar process: (1) preliminary identification of community housing needs using a variety of applied research methods including housing needs assessments, (2) development of an asset map and identification of resources, and (3) development and implementation of a community housing work plan. Through our research and experience working with community leaders, we have expanded on the steps in the Georgia Initiative for Community Housing program to provide the comprehensive steps used by communities with the best results.

National League of Cities Pilot Program

The elements of the community housing approach were first gleaned from the National League of Cities' Strengthening Partnerships for Housing Opportunities program (1998–2005). The program was a collaboration between the National League of Cities, the U.S. Department of Housing and

Urban Development, the National Affordable Housing Training Institute, and a consortium of public interest groups funded through a cooperative agreement with HUD (Imgrund, 1998). During its run, the program worked with four to eight cities, typically across two or three states within the same region, for 18 months. Like the housing team concept, participating cities brought together teams that included a cross-section of local players involved in housing and community development to foster a diversity of viewpoints (Imgrund, 1998). Local teams received consulting assistance from housing experts and National League of Cities staff, and technical assistance was provided at two regional housing conferences, one at the beginning and the other at the end of the program. The Georgia Municipal Association took part in the program in 2002. While challenges around affordable housing have escalated in recent years, many of the same problems experienced by small towns were voiced by communities participating in the National League of Cities program in the late 1990s and early 2000s. Difficulty in attracting developers to build affordable housing, a preponderance of substandard housing, infrastructure costs, and absentee landlords were commonly cited issues in smaller communities participating in the program.

While the Georgia Initiative for Community Housing program serves as the model for the community housing approach, other programs around the country are based on a similar model. MHP, a Minnesota-based community development organization, offers an 18-month, cohort-based Housing Institute for rural communities that shares many of the same features. The Rural Community Assistance Corporation's Tribal Housing Excellence Academy is a 30-month, cohort-based program designed to support tribal organizations in increasing their housing supply. Like the community housing approach, these programs are based on community development principles and a community-based model for addressing housing challenges. While structured programs similar to the community housing approach are limited, we recommend you inquire about participation if one is available to your community.

What the Community Housing Approach Is and Isn't

We have provided an overview of the community housing approach's components, history, and the theory underlying the approach. However, we understand that creating housing options can sometimes be met with misunderstandings and resistance. To avoid confusion, we would like to briefly summarize what is and is not part of the community housing approach.

The community housing approach *is*:

Based on basic community development principles. The approach we describe uses an asset-based community development framework as a foundation. Asset-based community development involves a process that boosts the ability of local leaders to work together and produces positive outcomes that affect participants and the community as a result of collective actions. For this reason, some of the elements of the blueprint may sound familiar. If your community is already engaged in one or more of the elements of the model, you are off to a good start! We hope that with examples from our experiences and research-based information, you can build on these elements and learn from communities that have experienced similar challenges.

A research-based approach. The community housing blueprint is informed by years of experience and research on the housing challenges faced by rural communities in Georgia and across the U.S. The approach results from our work with housing teams in the Georgia Initiative for Community Housing, insights gathered from community leaders in small towns nationwide, and a review of existing housing and community development research.

Supported by local government, but not only by local government. We use the term "community leaders" throughout this book, which may sound like another term for elected officials. Having the active engagement of one or more elected officials is essential. However, an effort led only by local government staff and elected officials can make meaningful change more difficult. The most successful housing efforts are led by a diverse group of people who have a stake in solving the community's housing challenges. Some people in the group may have a history of leadership in the community, while others may become leaders through their participation on the housing team.

Proactive, rather than reactive. The community housing approach is a conscious, active approach to charting a pathway to meeting community housing needs. The Eureka Moment is the realization and the pivot to action. The steps taken due to the Eureka Moment are all about being *proactive*.

An ongoing process. While housing initiatives are often time-limited, we have learned that the most successful communities view community housing as a continual process. Housing problems in rural America are many decades in the making. Adopting a community housing approach is an ongoing process because solving housing problems takes time and adaptation as local conditions change. One of the key changes the Georgia Initiative for Community Housing partners made when modeling a statewide program on the National League of Cities' program was to make it a three-year program. In 2020, requirements and incentives were added to encourage Georgia Initiative for Community Housing alumni communities to maintain their housing teams, keep an active work plan, and attend retreat sessions.

The community housing approach *is not*:

An anti-market approach. As discussed in the last chapter, relying solely on the private market to meet the community's housing needs is not a sustainable approach in the long run. However, this does not imply that we are against the private market. In fact, the private market has a significant role in the community housing approach. The difference between the two approaches—private market and community housing—is in who is responsible for the decision-making process and ensuring that new developments align with the community's housing needs. In some small towns, there has been no housing activity for a long time due to reliance on the private market. For these communities, attracting development could be a crucial objective. For other communities, collaboration with the private market will help fill the gaps in housing identified in the community's housing plan.

"Government housing." The mere mention of "government" and "housing" in the same sentence often evokes images of austere brick barracks and negative stereotypes of individuals who reside in public and subsidized housing. Although public housing owned and managed by housing authorities serves as a crucial source of housing, particularly for seniors in rural communities, we acknowledge that the stigma associated with government involvement often impedes housing provision for those who need it the most. The community housing approach collaborates with partners, including the local housing authority, to leverage federal programs such as federal and state Low Income Housing Tax Credits (LIHTC) and Community Development Block Grants (CDBG) to provide housing that caters to the community's needs.

Limited to housing low-income residents, rental housing, or homeownership. Community housing is about providing a diverse range of housing options for the whole community. All communities have gaps along the housing continuum. Rental housing affordable to low- and moderate-income households is a common gap, but not the only gap. Communities may also need an adequate supply of housing for first-time homeownership, appropriate housing for retirees, and market-rate rental housing. Bellehaven, for example, has worked on addressing existing housing in poor condition, providing market-rate multifamily rental housing, directing market-rate homeownership, and partnering with the local Habitat for Humanity to fill the gaps in the housing continuum.

Back to Bellehaven, Georgia

For the Bellehaven housing team, participation in the Georgia Initiative for Community Housing was a transformational experience. The housing team, led by the city's planning department, engaged the community, educated the political leaders, and provided regulatory revisions. Housing leaders formed a plan, established priorities, and initiated advocacy for housing opportunities.

Bellehaven recognized its housing challenges but first explored small footprint options within the community's comfort zone. The Downtown Development Authority, which used surplus land to pilot the development of a cluster of smaller houses, also proactively acquired land for affordable housing—first senior housing and then workforce housing. The housing team engaged in financial literacy programs, identified and leveraged local partnerships, and explored housing resources to address housing conditions. Recognizing that the most affordable housing unit is already standing, the team prioritized housing improvements by accessing housing rehabilitation funds. Bellehaven's Downtown Development Authority proactively courted multifamily infill options, attracting federal and state tax credit investors, and provided lots to Habitat for Humanity and local builders in exchange for workforce housing development agreements.

The community housing approach has been an ongoing process for Bellehaven. As some housing challenges are addressed, other problems emerge. The community is thriving and well-known for its classical homes and tourism industry. However, exurban migration, an escalating number of new home starts, and market-rate rents outpacing mortgages are a direct result of growth from more affluent residents moving into the community. Bellehaven's housing leadership faces these new challenges with the determination and flexibility to provide enduring, affordable, and accessible housing.

For communities of all sizes to thrive, there must be enough housing available for both owners and renters at various income levels that meet the needs of existing and future residents. Accomplishing this is especially challenging for small towns due to local governments' lower fiscal and administrative capacity and varying economic conditions (Lobao & Kelly, 2019). The community housing approach helps to address these limitations by leveraging the social capital available in small towns and rural areas. This approach draws on a community development model by bringing people in a community together to solve their local problems, improve their quality of life, and shape their future well-being. While communities participating in the Georgia Initiative for Community Housing program have the advantage of a structured program and the support of the state housing finance agency, the approach can be applied in individual communities that lack such support. In the following chapters, we expand on the approach by providing details, case examples, guiding questions, and tools to consider using.

Note

1 Bellehaven is a pseudonym. See Appendix for more information.

References

Brisson, D. (2009). Testing the relationship of formal bonding, informal bonding, and formal bridging social capital on key outcomes for families in low-income neighborhoods. *The Journal of Sociology & Social Welfare*, 36(1), 167–184. https://doi.org/10.15453/0191-5096.3411

Chaskin, R. J. (2001). Building community capacity: A definitional framework and case studies from a comprehensive community initiative. *Urban Affairs Review*, 36(3), 291–323. https://doi.org/10.1177/10780870122184876

Coleman, J. S. (1988). Social capital in the creation of human capital. *American Journal of Sociology*, 94, S95–S120. https://doi.org/10.1086/228943

Cook, C. C., Crull, S. R., Bruin, M. J., Yust, B. L., Shelley, M. C., Laux, S., Memken, J., Niemeyer, S., & White, B. J. (2009). Evidence of a housing decision chain in rural community vitality. *Rural Sociology*, 74(1), 113–137. https://doi.org/10.1526/003601109787524124

Häuberer, J. (2011). *Social capital theory towards a methodological foundation*. VS Verl. für Sozialwissenschaften.

Imgrund, J. (1998, June 1). Cities convene around housing issues. *Nation's Cities Weekly*, 21(22), 6.

Kennedy, M. (2007, April 22). From advocacy planning to transformative community planning. *Progressive City Magazine*. https://www.plannersnetwork.org/2007/04/from-advocacy-planning-to-transformative-community-planning/

Ling, C., & Dale, A. (2014). Agency and social capital: Characteristics and dynamics. *Community Development Journal*, 49(1), 4–20. https://doi.org/10.1093/cdj/bss069

Lobao, L., & Kelly, P. (2019). Local governments across the rural–urban continuum: Findings from a recent national county government study. *State and Local Government Review*, 51(4), 223–232. https://doi.org/10.1177/0160323X20922287

Mann, B. (2004, September 13). GMA models housing initiative on NLC program. *Nation's Cities Weekly*, 27(37), 5.

Morton, L. W., Allen, B. L., & Li, T. (2004). Rural housing adequacy and civic structure. *Sociological Inquiry*, 74(4), 464–491. https://doi.org/10.1111/j.1475-682X.2004.00101.x

Phillips, R., & Pittman, R. H. (Eds.). (2015). *An introduction to community development* (Second edition). Routledge.

Putnam, R. D. (1993). What makes democracy work? *National Civic Review*, 82(2), 101–107. https://doi.org/10.1002/ncr.4100820204

Putnam, R. D. (2001). *Bowling alone: The collapse and revival of American community* (1. Touchstone ed). Simon & Schuster [u.a.].

Tinsley, K., & Massey, J. (2009). The Georgia initiative for community housing. *Housing and Society*, 36(2), 195–211. https://doi.org/10.1080/08882746.2009.11430577

7

BUILDING A HOUSING TEAM

When rural communities form housing teams, they turn the spark of problem recognition into a firm foundation for making community-based housing decisions. This Eureka Moment is an inflection point. It is a milestone that initiates course correction to set a community on a different path. Creating a housing team transforms course correction into purposeful action by providing the structure to make decisions and plan for current and future housing needs. Housing teams shift the dynamic by sharing responsibility for housing in the community rather than fully relegating decisions to private market developers, builders, and landlords, who may reside outside the community and be primarily profit-based.

Housing teams perform the heavy lifting for the community housing approach. They plan, lead, and manage the process. They gather data and information, establish a vision and set goals, develop a plan, coordinate efforts to implement the plan, track progress, and maintain motivation for long-term success. Most importantly, they shoulder the responsibility of advocacy—education and engagement. The work of housing teams leads to two important outcomes: (1) housing decisions based on an expressed, shared vision and (2) the cultivation of local housing capacity.

DOI: 10.4324/9781003520450-7

Stakeholder-Driven Housing Teams Are the Foundation of Community Housing

Housing teams are formal working groups comprising people living or working in the community who are committed to addressing housing issues. They ideally include a wide range of community stakeholders, including staff and elected officials from municipal and county government, representatives from the school district, nonprofit housing, faith-based and other community organizations, or people working in the mortgage and banking industry, real estate agents, home builders, and property managers. Most importantly, housing teams include residents who bring different experiences and perspectives of the community. Stakeholder-driven housing teams provide a pool of individual skills and organizational strengths, which draw on and reinforce local networks of relationships, providing a richer and broader community resource for problem-solving. Housing team members become *community building organizers*, who design, implement, and manage the community housing effort (Mattessich & Monsey, 1997; Mattessich & Rausch, 2014). Housing team members are invested in community housing and willing to work to make it possible.

Representative stakeholder groups have become increasingly important in making decisions and implementing policies, especially as local governments recognize the value of shifting from traditional top-down approaches to more collaborative, community-focused governance (Beauregard, 1996; Pierre, 1999). A collaborative approach gives greater decision-making power to the individuals and communities directly impacted, resulting in a more responsive, community-focused way of approaching issues (Warner, 2003). The value of representative stakeholder groups literally resides in the knowledge and skills they contribute to the process, which leads to policies that address real needs on the ground. For this reason, stakeholder groups make a lot of sense for the community housing approach in small towns. A shift from private-sector led to community-based housing decision-making is unlikely to succeed without the participation of community members and resident groups. A stakeholder-led approach to housing leverages the human capital of small towns. By emphasizing involvement through housing teams, the community housing approach empowers communities to make decisions to improve their housing infrastructure through collaboration, community engagement, and locally based action.

Use of Stakeholder-Led Housing Teams Across Initiatives

Housing teams are the not-so-secret sauce of community housing initiatives. Drawing on the strengths, talents, and participation of a wide-ranging group of community members is not unique to Georgia's program nor the National League of Cities pilot program upon which it is based. In fact, the use of stakeholder-led teams is a common strategy among community planning initiatives. The Georgia Initiative for Community Housing is one of many programs that draw on a representative stakeholder model for housing planning. The *Housing Supply Accelerator* program developed by the National League of Cities and the American Planning Association emphasizes locally driven solutions through engaged stakeholders (Lowery et al., 2024). The Housing Assistance Council's (2025) *Technical Training and Assistance* program draws on organizational teams and the engagement of community partners to increase rural communities' capacity for housing, community, and economic development. The Minnesota Housing Partnership (MHP) (2025), a housing and community development organization, offers its *Housing Institute*, which provides a model similar to the Georgia Initiative for Community Housing, supporting community-based housing initiatives by combining a team-based approach using local stakeholders, curriculum to expand housing-based knowledge, and access to external networks on housing projects in rural Minnesota communities. While these examples include formal programs, the formation of stakeholder-led housing teams does not require a federal or statewide program. Because the stakeholder-driven teams are an integral element in community development practice, the approach is common among local housing initiatives and other community development efforts. In the following section, we provide tips for accessing information and technical assistance outside of a formal program.

Cultivating Local Housing Capacity Through Housing Teams

Rural communities must often cultivate the skills and knowledge needed to increase community capacity. Leadership and technical assistance initiatives have a strong track record of enhancing residents' skills and knowledge, contributing to stronger community capacity overall (Etuk et al., 2013).

At its core, the community housing approach is based on the premise that increasing community housing capacity is an efficient and effective way to address local housing needs. Stakeholder-led teams are mechanism for developing this capacity to address housing challenges and tackle development and planning issues (Naylor et al., 2021; Shucksmith, 2010; Skobba & Tinsley, 2016).

Key to this capacity-building process is the mobilization of social capital through local networks that leverage knowledge to address current and future needs (Shucksmith, 2010; Vasstrøm & Normann, 2019). Although rural communities may lack the trained planning professionals, housing expertise, and organizational networks found in larger cities, they often possess high levels of social capital, crucial for assembling a housing team of community stakeholders (Cook et al., 2009). Stakeholder-led teams engaged in housing decisions can streamline community planning and increase access to financial resources that are essential for improving housing and enhancing community vitality (Cook et al., 2009). Strong community norms, inclusive public dialogue, and high levels of communication enhance the ability of small towns to address housing adequacy challenges. Increasing the local capacity in this way is a form of community building (Mattessich, 2009; Morton et al., 2004).

The shift toward local, stakeholder-led approaches is connected to the aspects of social capital that facilitate coordination and cooperation for mutual benefit (Putnam, 1993). These attributes are associated with and fostered in rural communities, where tighter and smaller network relationships and proximity allow people to know one another, interact socially, and share organizational ties (Besser, 2009). Putnam (2001) views social capital as an essential characteristic of social life that enables participants to work together more effectively toward collective goals. It is a valuable resource for building the capacity needed for problem-solving and achieving those goals.

The Georgia Initiative for Community Housing program emphasizes building the capacity of housing teams to work on local housing challenges. Over the three years in the program, communities receive technical assistance at retreats to help local municipalities create and launch plans to address housing needs. Housing teams from various communities across the state come together at biannual retreats. These retreats provide opportunities to learn about innovative approaches and tap into resources for addressing housing and neighborhood challenges. The retreats also create by default a safe place beyond the community environs that enables housing teams to engage in frank dialogue without being in a fishbowl. By hosting expert speakers, connecting participants with resource representatives, peer learning, and fostering networking opportunities, the program aims to boost housing-related expertise and capacity while strengthening social connections at the community level.

These educational experiences and technical support empower communities to design and implement housing plans that meet their unique needs. During biannual retreats, participants dive into community development tools, such as federal funding programs, affordable housing development strategies, housing code enforcement, and housing needs assessments. Research on the program by Skobba and Tinsley (2016) has shown that involvement in the program significantly increases team members' capacity to use these tools and strategies effectively. By the third year in the program, participants often report greater expertise and more frequent use of critical community development tools than those just starting out.

While you may not have access to a program like the Georgia Initiative for Community Housing, you can build the capacity needed for your community. Finding people and resources that provide technical assistance will inform and empower your housing team. We have outlined a few sources below.

Find and reach out to communities that have had success working on housing issues. Talk with people at your state housing finance agency or search online to find rural or small towns in your state or neighboring states that have successfully worked on a housing. Peer learning is one of the most essential elements of the Georgia Initiative for Community Housing. It is also a relatively easy component to do on your own. In our experience, community leaders understand the challenges of working on housing issues and are willing to share their time and advice with fellow community leaders. Talking with a rural community that has attracted new workforce housing using the Low-Income Housing Tax Credit program, created loft housing in their downtown, or started a first-time homebuyer program can provide you with valuable information and inspiration. Take your housing team on a field trip if the community is nearby.

Access technical support offered by the county, region, and state. Many states have county extension offices offering programs, technical assistance, and housing and community development resources. Some states have regional planning commissions or organizations that serve rural areas. Your state housing finance agency, USDA regional Rural Development office, and statewide and national nonprofit housing and community development organizations offer technical assistance programs for rural communities. Technical assistance is also provided by intermediary organizations like Local Initiatives Support Coalition and Housing Assistance Council.

Utilize resources online. Several websites offer information about housing and community development tools and strategies. For example, the Local Housing Solutions website (localhousingsolutions.org) provides a wealth of information about housing planning, tools, and strategies in an accessible form. They also offer online training and provide technical assistance for a fee. The University of Kansas Center for Community Health and Development hosts a Community Tool Box website that provides information and toolkits on a wide range of applicable topics, including leadership, group facilitation, and problem-solving, how to assess community needs, strategic planning, and grant writing. These are just a few of the many resources available online.

Gaining access to existing knowledge will help you build the capacity to continue with steps in the community housing approach covered in the following three chapters. This support is crucial for overcoming resource limitations and bridging capacity gaps that can hinder housing efforts in small towns.

Getting Started: Forming a Housing Team in Your Community

The strength is that we all agree there is a problem. And they're all on the group to work. And they all bring something to the table.

GICH Housing Team Leader

If you are starting out, you may be wondering how to form a housing team. Who should be involved? How many people should be on the team? There is no one right way to form or make changes to housing teams. In the Georgia Initiative for Community Housing program, communities identify a representative group of stakeholders to serve on the community housing team. The teams include a mix of people representing municipal

Table 7.1 List of Potential Housing Team Members

Potential Housing Team Members	*Benefits to Team*
City and County Elected Officials	Elected officials bring political capital and decision-making authority. Often the local government is a utility provider as well, controlling infrastructure availability and service fees. City officials can help build public support, influence policy changes such as zoning amendments, and ensure housing initiatives are aligned with broader community priorities. County officials bring authority over county-level resources and can help align housing strategies with regional goals and funding streams. Many housing funding sources or investment incentives are primarily or exclusively available from, or held by, the local government or its agencies.
City and County Government Staff	Staff members bring expertise in planning, infrastructure, permitting, and code enforcement. They can provide technical guidance and help ensure that housing plans are realistic and actionable. City staff can provide continuity to a housing team, which may contribute to the sustainability of community housing initiatives. County staff can help integrate housing strategies with broader housing initiatives—county, region, and state.
Bank Representatives	Team members from the banking industry can provide insight into financing, lending, and credit availability. Their participation can open doors to innovative funding solutions and ensure housing projects align with financial realities.
Real Estate Professionals	Real estate agents offer firsthand knowledge of market conditions, property values, and consumer demand. They can identify opportunities for redevelopment and help bridge the gap between community goals and market trends.
Builders/ Developers	Developers and builders bring technical expertise in construction, site selection, and project management. They are aware of material and labor cost constraints and hurdles impacting the price and/or viability of housing. They can translate community visions into viable housing projects.

Table 7.1 (Continued)

Potential Housing Team Members	*Benefits to Team*
Nonprofit Organizations	Team members from nonprofit organizations bring community connections, service delivery expertise, and may have experience in grant writing and program management. They provide valuable information on unique housing tools such as land banks and land trusts. They can help ensure housing initiatives are equitable and inclusive.
Habitat for Humanity/ Nonprofit Housing Organizations	Nonprofit housing organizations, including Habitat for Humanity affiliates, have experience providing housing that meets community needs. Representatives from these organizations bring housing expertise as well as connections in the community. They can also speak to demand and credit challenges facing the community from a different perspective than real estate and banking professionals.
Public Housing Authorities (PHAs)	PHAs typically manage affordable housing and administer federal housing programs at the local level. They bring housing knowledge and an understanding of gaps in housing for lower income residents. PHAs are also able to issue bond instruments to finance affordable housing projects.
Local School Systems	Schools are directly impacted by housing stability, as student achievement is closely tied to secure housing. Team members from the local school district can provide valuable insight into how housing challenges affect children and families. School districts may also have land or existing buildings that could be used for housing.
Regional Planning/ Development Organizations	Regional agencies bring technical expertise in planning, data analysis, and access to federal or state resources. They help contextualize local housing efforts within a broader regional strategy.
Chambers of Commerce	The chamber connects housing to economic development. Businesses need a stable workforce, and chamber members can advocate for housing as a tool for economic vitality and growth. They can help collect information or anticipate demand for workforce housing.

Table 7.1 (Continued)

Potential Housing Team Members	*Benefits to Team*
Cooperative Extension	Extension agents provide educational resources, technical expertise, and community engagement experience. They can facilitate workshops, share research, and strengthen local capacity.
Residents	Residents offer lived experience and insight into the community's real housing challenges. Their voices ensure that housing solutions are grounded in everyday realities and have authentic community buy-in.
Faith-Based Organizations	Faith leaders bring trust, moral authority, and a strong network of volunteers. They often provide direct services such as shelter or food, making them vital partners in addressing housing insecurity. Faith-based organizations may have unskilled and skilled volunteer groups, maintain dedicated funds to address community needs, and engage in local mission work aligned with housing team priorities.
Economic Development, Downtown Development, Land Bank Authorities	These organizations focus on revitalization and economic growth. Their expertise in land assembly, redevelopment, and incentive structures can help unlock new opportunities for housing development.

Source: Authors.

and county government, residents, and people working in positions likely to have the knowledge and skills about housing and community needs, including mortgage and banking, real estate, school districts, nonprofit housing, and other community organizations and residents. Housing teams in the program typically have about 15 members. Housing team size will vary, but it is good to have a large enough team to divide the workload and small enough to have manageable meetings and committees.

Table 7.1 provides examples of potential housing team members and highlights the unique contributions each can offer to the process. While this list is not exhaustive, it serves as a valuable starting point for identifying who in your community should be at the table. Ultimately, each community must determine the right mix of stakeholders to build a team capable of addressing its specific housing needs.

Making Room at the Table

While social capital can strengthen communities and provide valuable resources, its effectiveness in addressing housing issues hinges on having a multitude of perspectives at the table. When forming housing teams, it is crucial to include people who have firsthand experience with the community's housing problems. If you only involve the usual stakeholders, your team may inadvertently push aside specific interests or create barriers that leave some groups out of the process (Besser, 2009; Putnam, 2001). Our statewide survey data revealed that people most in need of housing and those who are most familiar with the community's housing challenges (school representatives and community organizations) are often sidelined from housing discussions in small towns (Odeyemi & Skobba, 2021). As Latimer (2022) argues in *Small Isn't Beautiful: The Case Against Localism*, decisions made at the local level often result in poor and unjust outcomes. The U.S. has a long history of local-level housing decisions that have limited access to housing and other community resources through racial and socio-economic segregation (Kahlenberg, 2023). Local decision-making is typically less focused on actual housing needs in the community and more about reinforcing the status quo. Housing teams that represent diverse viewpoints within the community can challenge and change the status quo by increasing housing options.

City, County, or Region? Considering Your Housing Team's Service Area

Throughout this book, we have talked about rural communities and small towns and have used this term interchangeably with community. Many people working on housing issues in rural areas work in county government or for an organization serving multiple cities or counties. If you are considering implementing a community housing approach, we recommend starting with one municipality within the county or your service area. There are several reasons for this approach. Working within one city or town will make it easier to garner political will and community buy-in. Residents are attached to and care about their community. Working with more than one community or at the county level can make it harder for housing teams to coalesce and manage the different aspects of the community housing approach. The limited geographic area of small towns combined with municipal government planning and decision-making will make any community housing initiative more manageable. It is helpful to have county-level government and agencies represented on your housing team, and they may even be collaborating partners on a community-focused initiative. If you pursue a county-led initiative, we recommend you start by focusing on one municipality. Pay close attention to Chapter 8, which covers political will and community support, to ensure everyone is on the same page before forming a housing team.

Lessons Learned from Effective Housing Teams

Our research and observation of housing teams suggest that there is no one perfect way to form a housing team. Successful housing teams include a combination of the roles and expertise. Insights from our research suggest that finding people who can provide different perspectives, including people who do not have formal power or who are not part of the power structure of the community is important. While it helps to have people with experience in housing, it is not necessary for success.

Communities that have proved successful in achieving their goals during the program and have longevity beyond the third year of the program share the following characteristics.

Leadership or active involvement of local government. Participation from local government staff and elected officials is vital for several reasons. Local governments have access to state and federal funding sources and are instrumental in public-private partnerships to develop housing. Having a community housing initiative led or officially endorsed by local government is also helpful where housing efforts require changes in zoning regulations. Including team members from local government can also provide continuity and allow for succession planning for your housing team.

A variety of stakeholders who bring different perspectives, skill sets, and expertise. Housing teams that experienced success in the Georgia Initiative for Community Housing program included people working in various organizations and from different stakeholder groups. What this mix of people looks like varies by community. Why does variety matter for housing teams? Small-town housing teams comprising entirely or mostly local government members tend to be formulaic, lacking the creativity and passion required for a sustained community housing initiative. Grassroots housing teams have the energy, passion, and understanding of community needs that may lead to success in the short term but can be hard to sustain. A housing team led by people who work in the housing arena, particularly if the group comprises people working in the private market, is more likely to produce the status quo.

Team members who share a commitment to improving housing conditions and view the initiative as a long-term endeavor. The passion and dedication of team members are as important as the skills and expertise they bring to the table. Successful housing teams include members who express a strong desire to participate in housing initiatives and see the work as more than a time-limited program or one-time effort. These team members build strong bridges that will be traversed more than once; they are invested in sustained success. Strong team members recognize that meaningful change takes time and persistent effort. They are committed to housing improvement as a long-term community goal.

Flexibility and adaptability to changing circumstances. This characteristic embodies a proactive and flexible approach to problem-solving and responding to evolving team needs and changing dynamics. This trait is particularly relevant to adapting to changes within housing team composition. Recruitment is an ongoing activity in effective housing teams, as is education. Over time, the composition of housing teams changes. The large group who initially volunteered will change as you get started. People attend a few meetings and then drop off. Gaps in representation or expertise are identified, and new people join the team. Being open and flexible to organizational change is key to having a resilient team that can sustain itself through the good and hard times that come with implementing a community housing approach.

Regular meetings and responsibility assignments. Consistent meetings lead to steady progress. When meetings drop off, activity drops off. It is also better in this hectic modern world to schedule regular meetings so that the team members commit to regular block on their calendars, and then cancel a meeting when there is no business that requires immediate action.

Team members are also more likely to stay engaged and attend meetings if they have a specific responsibility. Team members are either volunteering their time or taking on an additional role as part of their job. With clear roles and responsibilities, time spent as a housing team member is more likely to feel worth the effort. Remember meaningful work matters.

Effective leaders who cultivate talent and share responsibility for achieving goals. Our research on housing teams highlights the critical role of team leaders. Successful housing teams have leaders who are good communicators. Like other strong team members, they share a sincere commitment to addressing housing challenges. Effective team leaders are relationship-builders who foster trusting relationships with team members and draw on the collective strengths of the team to accomplish goals while also forging connections outside of the community. They ensure that all team members have a meaningful role and proactively cultivate leadership skills and potential within the team. In this manner, effective leaders contribute to housing team success and sustainability.

Strategies for Building and Sustaining a Housing Team

Working with and sustaining any community-led action group can be even more difficult. People move or change jobs. Lives become busier. Over the following pages, we will share strategies for building and maintaining successful housing teams and a few lessons learned on things to avoid. These strategies are based on findings from our case study research on rural and small-town housing teams participating in the Georgia Initiative for Community Housing as well as tips and lessons from our experience working with the program and housing teams over many years.

This chapter underscores the vital role of housing teams and housing team characteristics in designing, developing, and implementing a community housing approach. When combined with strong local relationships, a housing team's collective skills and organizational strengths become the backbone for working on housing challenges within the community. An effective housing team ensures the community housing approach is implemented strategically and meets goals, while also being able to weather changes and barriers. In a few chapters, we will explore the housing team's crucial tasks—gathering data, coordinating efforts, developing plans, and tracking progress.

References

Beauregard, R. A. (1996). City planning and the postwar regime in Philadelphia. In Mickey Lauria (Ed.), *Reconstructing urban regime theory* (pp. 171–188). Sage Books.

Besser, T. L. (2009). Changes in small town social capital and civic engagement. *Journal of Rural Studies*, 25(2), 185–193. https://doi.org/10.1016/j.jrurstud.2008.10.005

Cook, C. C., Crull, S. R., Bruin, M. J., Yust, B. L., Shelley, M. C., Laux, S., Memken, J., Niemeyer, S., & White, B. J. (2009). Evidence of a housing decision chain in rural community vitality. *Rural Sociology*, 74(1), 113–137. https://doi.org/10.1526/003601109787524124

Etuk, L. E., Rahe, M. L., Crandall, M. S., Sektnan, M., & Bowman, S. (2013). Rural leadership development: Pathways to community change. *Community Development*, 44(4), 411–425. https://doi.org/10.1080/15575330.2012.761639

Housing Assistance Council. (2025). *Training and technical assistance*. Housing Assistance Council. https://ruralhome.org/our-work/technical-assistance/

Kahlenberg, R. D. (2023). *Excluded: How snob zoning, NIMBYism, and class bias build the walls we don't see* (First edition). Public Affairs.

Latimer, T. (2022). *Small isn't beautiful: The case against localism*. Brookings Insitution Press.

Lowery, L., Wallace, M., Jordan, J., Pasi, E., Lang, L., Onuaja, S., & Chapman, M. (2024). *Housing supply accelerator playbook*. National League of Cities and American Planning Association. https://www.nlc.org/resource/housing-supply-accelerator-playbook/

Mattessich, P. (2009). Social capital and community building. In R. Phillips & R. H. Pittman (Eds.), *An introduction to community development* (pp. 49–57). Routledge.

Mattessich, P., & Monsey, B. (1997). *Community building: What makes it work*. Amherst H. Wilder Foundation.

Mattessich, P. W., & Rausch, E. J. (2014). Cross-sector collaboration to improve community health: A view of the current landscape. *Health Affairs*, 33(11), 1968–1974. https://doi.org/10.1377/hlthaff.2014.0645

Minnesota Housing Partnership (MHP). (2025). *Housing Institute*. Minnesota Housing Partnership (MHP). https://mhponline.org/housing-institute/

Morton, L. W., Allen, B. L., & Li, T. (2004). Rural housing adequacy and civic structure. *Sociological Inquiry*, 74(4), 464–491. https://doi.org/10.1111/j.1475-682X.2004.00101.x

Naylor, R. S., Hunt, C. A., & Zimmerer, K. S. (2021). Bridging the troubled waters of tourism studies: From social capital and rural community development to livelihood sovereignty. *International Journal of Tourism Anthropology*, 8(4), 370. https://doi.org/10.1504/IJTA.2021.123199

Odeyemi, E., & Skobba, K. (2021). Who is at the table? Civic engagement in small town housing decision-making. *Local Government Studies*, 47(6), 1014–1036. https://doi.org/10.1080/03003930.2020.1864334

Pierre, J. (1999). Models of urban governance: The institutional dimension of urban politics. *Urban Affairs Review*, 34(3), 372–396. https://doi.org/10.1177/10780879922183988

Putnam, R. D. (2001). *Bowling alone: The collapse and revival of American community* (1. Touchstone ed). Simon & Schuster [u.a.].

Shucksmith, M. (2010). Disintegrated rural development? Neo-endogenous rural development, planning and place-shaping in diffused power contexts. *Sociologia Ruralis*, 50(1), 1–14. https://doi.org/10.1111/j.1467-9523.2009.00497.x

Skobba, K., & Tinsley, K. (2016). Addressing housing and neighborhood revitalization needs in Georgia's rural and small towns: A study of the Georgia Initiative for Community Housing. *Community Development*, 47(4), 449–463. https://doi.org/10.1080/15575330.2016.1205117

Vasstrøm, M., & Normann, R. (2019). The role of local government in rural communities: Culture-based development strategies. *Local Government Studies*, 45(6), 848–868. https://doi.org/10.1080/03003930.2019.1590200

Warner, M. E. (2003). Competition, cooperation, and local governance. In D. L. Brown, L. E. Swanson, & A. W. Barton (Eds.), *Challenges for rural America in the twenty-first century* (pp. 252–261). Pennsylvania State University Press.

8

GAINING POLITICAL WILL AND COMMUNITY BUY-IN

On the surface, the defeat of proposed housing due to community opposition can look like a simple process. A new housing development is proposed. Residents show up and voice their objections. The zoning board, city council, or county commissioners reject the plan. In reality, the path to defeat starts long before the meeting. It begins when key decision makers remain actively or passively uncommitted to housing plans and when plans move forward without engaging residents in the process. Successful community housing initiatives start with two key ingredients—political will and community support. Political will is when key decision-makers commit to supporting a specific solution for a given problem (Post et al., 2010). Community support, or buy-in, is the active backing of a plan or solution by residents who understand the benefits and feel a sense of ownership because they were included in the process (Wilcox, 2022).

Overlooking the need for political will or community buy-in can result in the slowing down or halting of community housing efforts. We have witnessed years of work wash away when differing political goals or

DOI: 10.4324/9781003520450-8

community opposition derail a housing team's efforts. While residents are the most common source of opposition, community leaders can also withdraw support or even actively oppose plans for housing that were years in the making (Scally, 2014b). Lack of community support for housing receives more media attention, though a lack of political will is often a more significant barrier to progress. These two crucial forms of support are interrelated. "Not in my backyard," or NIMBY, opposition is more likely to be swift and effective without political will signaled by solid, authentic support from local leadership. With political will in place, community leaders can engage residents, addressing and potentially pre-empting community opposition to housing or redirecting their focus from opposition to mitigation. When housing plans have both political will and community buy-in, everyone is moving in the same direction.

From Promise to Pushback: Sweetwater's Housing Effort Unraveled

A case study of Sweetwater,[1] a small town with about 2,500 residents in southeastern Georgia, illustrates the interrelated role that political will and community support play in housing initiatives. When Sweetwater applied for the Georgia Initiative for Community Housing program, it had all the components for a successful community-led effort. Community leaders in Sweetwater had experienced the Eureka Moment after recognizing that the lack of housing affordable to low- and middle-income households was a barrier to new business investment. The housing team had data to back their claims. The community entered the program with support from city and county governments, a skilled and passionate leader, and a robust housing team comprising a well-represented stakeholder group. Most of the Sweetwater housing team attended the first program retreat. At the second retreat six months later, the team had dwindled to a few members. During the intervening six months, the group had undergone several changes. The dynamic housing team leader, who was instrumental in forming the housing team and submitting their application to the Georgia Initiative for Community Housing program, had taken a job in another state. A local election brought a new mayor. Most of the original team members departed along with the former team leader and the previous mayor.

Despite its diminished size, the Sweetwater housing team engaged a nonprofit developer for a proposed Low Income Housing Tax Credit (LIHTC) development. The project plans included a mix of market rate and affordable rental housing. A story about the proposed housing development ran in the local newspaper, and the plans moved forward until the development's proposed rezoning came up for consideration at a zoning board meeting. A standing-room-only crowd of residents showed up to oppose the rezoning for the housing development. Concerned residents stated a predictable list of concerns—traffic, crime, and property values. But they had other concerns as well. Residents felt blindsided by the proposed development. They questioned the need for affordable housing and expressed concern about the lack of communication regarding the development. The day after this contentious meeting, the developer pulled the project's LIHTC application, the primary source of project funding, from consideration. Community opposition had been swift and effective in halting plans that addressed the very housing problems the Sweetwater team had identified and sought to solve. Sweetwater's experience is not unique. Proposed housing developments are most likely to face opposition early in the process—after a developer is engaged and a site is selected but before zoning changes and building permit approvals are issued (Scally, 2014a).

As housing becomes more expensive and harder to find, a wider range of Americans view the lack of housing affordability and availability as a serious problem locally and nationally. Most Americans in rural and urban areas will readily agree that we need to build more homes to buy and rent (Radosevich & Turner, 2024). Considering this broad agreement, gaining local support for new housing should be easy. But it isn't. At least not yet. The road to political will and community support for housing is long and filled with detours and potholes. Community leaders and residents alike may acknowledge the need for more housing options, yet acknowledgment is not the same as support. Local recognition of housing problems is frequently coupled with resistance to building the needed housing (Adams et al., 2023; Marble & Nall, 2017).

Pulling in the Same Direction: Establishing Political Will

Building local political will is not an easy task. It requires community leaders to share an understanding of the problem and an agreement about possible solutions. Achieving this common ground can be complicated by a reluctance to lean away from the "private market can do it better" ethos and conflicting ideas about what housing the community needs or wants, especially if solutions include housing for low-income residents (Osinubi et al., 2022). For decision-makers seeking solutions to housing challenges, limited population size and close, interconnected social relationships in small towns can present barriers (Oliver, 2012). The proximity to constituents, who are also the people they see in the grocery store, local businesses, church, and at community events, makes it risky to support solutions that may be unpopular (Catlaw & Stout, 2016; Trautman, 2016). Additionally, local government is layered with different players, including city and county staff, commissioners and city council members, mayors, zoning boards, and the boards of education, who influence different aspects of housing development. Fractures in political will often stem from disagreement within and between government entities. For municipalities and counties, differing views about housing are common, especially when one entity is the sole utility provider. Within government differences can also weaken political will. Lack of support may stem from elected officials with differing viewpoints or staff members who undercut housing initiatives by slow walking information, missing deadlines, and disparaging projects in behind-the-scenes conversations with elected officials. Disparate views of how things ought to be can quickly undermine much-needed political will when shifting to a community housing approach.

Overcoming the barriers that undermine political will is crucial to a successful community housing approach. Given the numerous challenges, how do communities establish the political will needed for housing? Garnering political will requires a critical mass of decision-makers who share a common understanding of local housing problems and are willing to publicly commit to agreed-upon solutions, and a strong base of community support (Catlaw & Stout, 2016; Post et al., 2010; Trautman, 2016). Political will among decision-makers and community support among residents are different but interrelated processes. Yet having the tools to recognize resistance and build a base of support are fundamental to both.

Elements Required for Political Will

Before we dive into the signs of decision-maker resistance and tips to help get everyone on the same page, we thought it would be helpful to know what political will requires. Knowing the makings of political will can be the difference between knowing when you are in a strong position to propose housing changes and when you have more foundational work to do.

Post et al. (2010) identified four elements required for political will:

1. **There is a critical mass of supportive decision-makers.** Understanding when you have enough support requires that you know who has decision-making power and whether you have enough of this group on board. In small towns, this group of decision-makers can consist of city and county staff, elected officials, school boards, and planning commissions. However, there may be other community leaders with significant influence. It also requires awareness of who is and is not supportive. Which decision-makers recognize the community's housing challenges and are supportive of the community housing team's objectives and plan? Who might actively or passively oppose your work?
2. **Decision-makers agree on the problem and are willing to acknowledge it publicly.** Having support from a sufficient group of community leaders is only helpful if these decision-makers are on the same page about the problem. Additionally, behind-the-scenes support is not always adequate to the task at hand. Elected officials and staff must be willing to publicly acknowledge the issue in city council or county commission meeting agendas, resolutions, and other formal processes.
3. **Decision-makers must be genuinely committed to supporting proposed housing solutions.** Reaching a critical mass of supportive decision-makers is only useful when support is authentic. Housing can be divisive, especially when plans include affordable housing, rental options, or even multifamily density for higher income residents. This can make it challenging to detect superficial commitment. Public statements and actions consistent with proposed housing solutions are indicators of genuine commitment. We provide other ways to detect decision-maker resistance a little later in this chapter.
4. **Decision-makers are in general agreement about a proposed approach, which will realistically address housing problems.** This fourth component recognizes that political will requires decision-makers to be on the same page about potentially feasible solutions to addressing housing problems. Decision-makers do not need to agree

on all the details, but they do need to agree on the proposed approach as the way to move forward. The proposed approach must be *potentially effective*, meaning proposed solutions are not "pie in the sky" plans or superficial fixes that will do little to resolve acknowledged housing problems.

It is not enough for a small group of community leaders to understand, support, and act on housing needs. Applying Post et al.'s (2010) four elements of political will helps to ensure that key decision-makers are included in discussions early on and that everyone is on the same page about the problem and potential solutions.

Deficits in political will can quickly derail community housing efforts. We have observed communities in the Georgia Initiative for Community Housing program begin with a robust housing team and clear work plan, only to hit political will roadblocks a year or two later. We have watched cracks in support and consensus become deep, sometimes permanent, divisions between housing team members, elected officials, or both, and housing plans disrupted as critical decision-makers, excluded from early planning efforts, voice opposition during discussions about a proposed housing development.

Political Will Fault Lines

The Foothills County[2] housing team illustrates how missing elements of political will can impede progress. Foothills County entered the Georgia Initiative for Community Housing program with a housing team comprising key decision-makers from the county and community leaders from local businesses, social services, nonprofit, and faith-based organizations. The team's housing work plan reflected a rural county experiencing growth due to combination of local natural amenities, access to jobs, and urbanization. The county needed high-quality rental apartments affordable to the local workforce and they had identified a target area for development. The Foothills County housing team made progress on several priorities, including addressing substandard housing conditions, but the development of new apartments remained an elusive goal. The target development area was within one of the county's small towns. Decision-makers for this small town were not part of the housing team and they did not want rental apartments in their community. The inability to make progress on this key housing priority slowed but did not stop the team. The Foothills County team recalibrated its approach. They conducted a housing needs assessment for all the municipalities in the county. They used the results as a starting point for discussions with leaders and staff in each community. This process helped to garner political will among leaders and seven years after starting the Georgia Initiative for Community Housing program, new affordable rental apartments opened in the target area identified by the Foothills County housing team.

Getting (and keeping) everyone on the same page regarding housing is both difficult and necessary. This challenge is often more complex when trying to negotiate consensus among city and county government leaders, who often have divergent and even competitive interests. Yet, working together, city and county leaders can form powerful and effective community housing teams. Counties generally control water and sewer systems, while municipalities control where the land uses are more concentrated and have more robust service-delivery that makes it possible. You need both to create new housing.

The Pushback and Passivity That Undermine Political Will

Recognizing the Characters: Typology of Resistant and Uncommitted Decision-Makers

Monica has spent *a lot* of time attending city council, zoning board, and housing commission meetings —enough time to readily identify when community leaders are not on board. A natural at reading people and a qualitative researcher at heart, Monica has made good use of her countless hours in meetings, using her observational skills and sense of humor to develop an informal typology of decision-maker personality types. Her typology offers a lighthearted way to identify the uncommitted, the people who lack the political will or investment needed to be counted among your decisive decision-makers.

The Nostalgist ("Back-in-My-Dayer")

The Nostalgist longs for the way things used to be. They champion the good ol' way, even when it no longer fits the present day. They resist change not because they oppose housing, but because they fear what new development might mean for the community's identity. Their vision is rooted in the past, making it difficult to plan for the future.

The Budget Hawk ("Bean Counter in Chief")

The Budget Hawk, also known as the Bean Counter in Chief, focuses solely on fiscal restraints, viewing housing initiatives as a drain on public resources. Their concern for cost overshadows concern for need. They can oppose funding studies, hiring consultants, or allocating staff time—even when those investments are modest and strategic.

The Passive Partner ("Major Meh")

The Passive Partner, technically part of the housing team but true to their Major Meh moniker, is an acknowledged seat warmer. Perhaps they are a political designee or a performative representative. They may attend meetings but rarely contribute. Their silence can be mistaken for agreement, but it is actually a lack of investment, robbing the housing discussion of helpful contributions.

The Ideologue ("Captain Conviction")

The Ideologue is guided more by personal beliefs than by housing data. They may affirm a deep commitment to rural or small-town character or may be firmly opposed to public intervention, but their worldview leaves little room for compromise. Even when polite, they can be impervious to facts and immovable roadblocks for housing compromises.

The White Knight ("Councilmember Crusader")

This decision-maker type prides themselves on being in touch with the community—but only a narrow slice of it. They often echo growth concerns of the loudest voices at public meetings, willingly neglectful of the broader community's housing needs. Lending a favored ear to the usual suspects, they can base decisions on prevailing public opinion, not public need.

The Fence Sitter ("Mayor Maybe")

The Fence Sitter is reluctant to take a stand on housing issues because they are torn by competing interests or even always see both sides. They may agree with the need for housing but fear backlash from vocal constituents. Their indecisiveness can stall forward movement, especially when their vote or voice is needed to move a plan forward.

The Can Kicker ("Clerk of Tomorrow Town")

The Can Kicker acknowledges housing is a problem, yet invariably insists now is not the time to act. They prefer to address the issue... eventually. Can Kickers defer decisions, awaiting more data, more funding, or more consensus? They are not opposed; they simply are not ready to commit—often undermining team cohesion or commitment and resulting in abandonment.

The Wild Card ("Agent of Chaos")

The Wild Card decision-maker is not opposed to housing solutions but their approach leaves others spinning. They may propose unconventional ideas or alliances, enjoy heated arguments, or have a dramatic flair—think bow-ties and big hats, bold metaphors, and surprise slide decks. Unpredictable, they can bring refreshing creativity or derail structured conversations.

The Lone Ranger ("Sheriff Self-Reliance")

This decision-maker resists collaborative planning for housing, championing self-sufficiency and personal responsibility. The Lone Ranger's deep belief in independence may conflict with any collective effort needed for community housing initiatives. They are unlikely to support housing strategies involving subsidies, partnerships, or shared infrastructure.

The Predictability of Resistance to Change

Understanding underlying motivations is key to working with local government leaders, housing team members, and residents who undermine the ability to foster the political will and community support needed to respond to housing issues. Resistance to change is common and predictable. People react to change in different, recognizable ways that are influenced by cognitive, emotional, and behavioral factors. For instance, individuals, which roughly align with our *Nostalgist, Budget Hawk*, and *Passive Partner* decision-makers, illustrate how personality traits and long-held ways of thinking underlie resistance to change (Pardo Del Val & Martínez Fuentes, 2003). These three types include people who prefer to:

- Seek routine, stability, and predictability (*The Nostalgist*)
- Focus on short-term, immediate costs over long-term benefits (*The Budget Hawk*)
- Avoid engaging deeply with new ideas (*The Passive Partner*).

People with these underlying preferences may not be overtly oppositional, but their behaviors—whether rooted in nostalgia, fiscal conservatism, or disengagement—can stall or even derail your housing efforts.

Resistance to change occurs both actively and passively. Active resistance is easier to identify because it appears as overt, vocal opposition. For example, the *Ideologue* and *White Knight* may vigorously advocate for deeply held beliefs or a favored constituency to override data-driven planning. People who are passive in their resistance to change delay or disengage without open confrontation (Pardo Del Val & Martínez Fuentes, 2003). The *Fence-Sitter's* and *Can-Kicker's* passivity, whether due to a reluctance to commit in the face of competing pressures or fear of public backlash, results in undermining team progress. Passive resistance can be harder to identify and slower to reveal itself, making it problematic when trying to build political will. And even the more colorful characters, like the *Wild Card* or *Loan Ranger*, conceal resistance through unpredictability or hyper-individualism, which challenge collaborative, community-based approaches. Resistance may be compounded by uncertainty, perceived workload, or lack of trust in leadership (Khaw et al., 2023).

Working with Resistant and Reluctant Decision-Makers

By recognizing the archetypes of common and well-documented resistance patterns, you can better anticipate and navigate resistance that undermines political will. Understanding people and their motivations enables you to approach resistance with empathy and foresight, proving far more strategic than dismissal or frustration. Awareness can also empower your team to self-diagnose and tactically avoid the perils of resistance. If you see any of these characters among your group of decision-makers or along your housing journey, you have some work to do building political will.

Coming to a clear understanding of how leaders view the problem and potential solutions will help identify decision hurdles. You may need to gather more information or bring in the perspective of other organizations or community leaders. To develop political will, you may need to not only hear, but also listen to the voices of people who will be part of your community housing team. You may also need to gather some data before defining the problem and desired outcomes. If your community lacks a sufficient supply of modest-priced rental housing, but some community leaders want to increase homeownership opportunities to attract higher income households, discussing and prioritizing these housing challenges is essential prior to developing the messages needed to establish community buy-in. It is difficult to quell community opposition to housing if the call is coming from inside the house.

Community Support: The Cornerstone of Political Will

The Sweetwater housing team understood the housing problems facing the community and they had researched solutions. Despite the loss of key housing team leaders, they had identified available land and attracted a developer who was planning to build the very housing the community needed—a significant accomplishment for a small town of less than 3,000 residents. Yet, the Sweetwater housing team lacked a critical mass of support and influence needed to establish political support. They also overlooked the crucial role that community support plays in resident and decision-maker support for affordable housing. When residents showed up en masse to oppose the proposed development, even if elected officials personally supported the housing development, the lack of public support would have made it difficult to do anything other than oppose the efforts of the housing team. In the end, the swift community opposition not only shut down the proposed development in Sweetwater but also ended the journey of their housing team.

Community Support and Opposition

Community support goes beyond *acceptance* or a willingness to go along with a proposal to visible support for a project, plan, or initiative (Poulsen et al., 2014). Community support means that residents recognize the intended benefit of the proposal and feel a sense of ownership because they have been part of the decision-making process (Wilcox, 2022). Our approach to community buy-in starts with the perspective that the residents are the experts for their communities. Community members need to be included in conversations about housing challenges early in the process, represented in the planning process, listened to when they voice concerns, and given straightforward and honest information about how concerns will be addressed. We acknowledge that developing local support for community housing takes time. Investing time to bring the community into the conversation is time well spent. As the Sweetwater case highlights, failing to engage the community early can result in opposition that quickly and decisively halts efforts and slows momentum.

Community opposition to proposed housing is common and examples are easy to find. A quick search online will turn up local stories of resident opposition to a wide range of housing plans, from affordable rental housing to high-priced, owner-occupied townhomes. As implied by the phrase associated with the acronym, NIMBY, opposition is often associated with self-interest. Residents who oppose unwanted development are often considered uninformed or selfish (Burningham, 2000; Freudenburg & Pastor, 1992). The reasoning goes something like this. If more affordable housing for workers is needed, people who create barriers must not understand the problem (the uninformed). If they understand the problem, they are impeding housing plans out of self-interest or a lack of empathy (the selfish). Sit in on any public hearing about proposed workforce housing, and you will likely hear community members with opposing viewpoints describe their take on the issue or call out the views of others using these perspectives. These negative views of the public are not likely to yield success in building community support.

Fostering community support for housing requires understanding how residents think about and value their community's physical and social character. The communities we live in hold significant meaning in our lives and are connected to our sense of self and personal identities (Proshansky et al.,

1983). People form emotional connections, or place attachments, with their homes, neighborhoods, and communities (Manzo, 2003; Manzo & Perkins, 2006). Place attachments tend to grow stronger the longer one lives in a place, affecting thoughts, feelings, beliefs, and actions (and reactions) about local communities (Manzo & Perkins, 2006). People with strong attachments to the community are more likely to take an interest in what is happening at the local level and take action when proposed changes are inconsistent with their beliefs and perceptions than those with weaker place attachments (Devine-Wright, 2009).

Community opposition is a place-based protective response activated when new development threatens place-based attachments and identities (Devine-Wright, 2009). Residents' concerns typically focus on a predictable set of anticipated problems that new housing developments may cause, including increased crime, declining property values, school capacity issues, and traffic (Ault, 2015). While these concerns are understandable, they also reflect worries about how proposed changes will disrupt place attachments by affecting the familiarity of the place or community (Eranti, 2017). Community character and identity influence and are influenced by new development and land use changes (Alkon & Traugot, 2008). The smaller the pond the bigger the ripple feels. Any potential changes to the physical landscape will be filtered through residents' perceptions of and attachments to the community.

While writing this chapter, I (Kim) thought of my childhood home. In 1970, my family moved to a small subdivision in the rural, unincorporated part of Prior Lake, Minnesota. My neighborhood was a small island of houses surrounded by picturesque farms. Getting to the nearest large city or the interstate meant traveling along narrow, winding roads, some made of gravel. Today, Prior Lake has nearly 30,000 residents and is part of the expanding contiguous suburbs south of Minneapolis. However, in the 1970s, it had a population of about 4,000. As a young child, I appreciated the view of the beautiful, rural landscape as I looked down the street, just beyond John Deere Drive. When I think about place attachment, I think about the land and vista of my childhood home. Had development of this land been proposed back then, my emotional connection to this landscape would have made acceptance difficult. I imagine my parents and neighbors lining up to complain about how this new housing or commercial development was ruining the community's rural character. While local housing challenges do not always involve changes to the physical landscape, understanding the power of place attachment and the aspects of the built environment residents value will be helpful as you begin planning for community housing.

Building Community Support for Housing

Small towns possess many components needed to build the community support for a sustainable community housing model, including strong social ties, frequent interactions, and social norms supporting civic life. However, community leaders and residents alike can resist new housing development, particularly when they have been left out of the process. Gaining buy-in for community housing involves providing multiple chances for residents to identify needs and opportunities and suggest possible solutions to address them (Wilcox, 2022). The engagement required to develop community support requires a significant time investment.

If you have reached the Eureka Moment by realizing your community has one or more housing problems, you are probably eager to start working on solutions. Housing problems, once recognized, have a sense of urgency because they affect the lives of residents and the community as a whole. We encourage you to take time to build community support before making any plans. If community members are first learning about proposed housing at a meeting where a developer is presenting well-defined plans, you have not adequately involved residents in the process.

Below, we offer steps to consider when building community support. Some of these steps include good resources on community engagement, which are included in the references at the end of this chapter.

Prepare for community engagement. Develop a community engagement plan that includes strategies to reach a wide range of people from the community. You probably have a list of "the regulars"—the 7–10 people who usually show up, provide input, and are at the table when decisions are made. Bringing in new voices is essential to garnering community support. A community engagement plan outlines strategies to reach people who will provide different perspectives and viewpoints. Conducting a stakeholder analysis can help you identify whom you need to reach and how you will reach them.

Provide opportunities for community members to provide input about the problems and share ideas about solutions. Starting with conversations among small groups of residents with different perspectives is a good first step (Ault, 2015). Small groups make it easier to connect with individuals in the community and hear what they have to say. People are more likely to speak in small groups than in large meetings. Starting with a large group can be intimidating for leaders as well as participants and can lead to a discussion dominated by detractors. After utilizing small group discussion, consider other forms of gathering input from residents, including community forums, surveys, focus groups, and visioning sessions.

By building trust and encouraging active participation, community leaders can engage and empower residents to share their insights, propose innovative ideas, and work together to develop practical, community-driven solutions (Abt Associates & NYU Furman Center, 2026). Community leaders should also be transparent about how they will use community input in decision-making as well as when and how residents will have additional opportunities to participate or provide feedback on proposed plans (Abt Associates & NYU Furman Center, 2026).

Identify, acknowledge, and address concerns. Identifying and acknowledging concerns early in the process is vital when implementing a community housing approach. As the Sweetwater case highlights, residents do not appreciate learning about plans at the first formal hearing. In the report "Building Support for Affordable Housing," Ault (2015) recommends asking community members, sometimes repeatedly, why they are concerned about the proposed plan or project. Asking residents questions about their concerns can help them get beyond surface concerns and uncover the root causes. For example, opposition to high-density development might be expressed as concerns about overcrowding when the root issue is the desire to preserve open spaces. Identifying these deeper reasons can lead to housing solutions which could also address the detracting concern as well.

Understand community values and develop messaging that speaks to these values. Examining the core values that shape public attitudes and opinions will help you understand how people in the community weigh and approach housing issues (Belden et al., 2003). We have identified common mindsets that may influence attitudes, but people in your community likely hold additional or more specific values. Residents are less likely to oppose a plan when messaging is framed in terms of their values (Belden et al., 2003). Buy-in occurs when people clearly understand the intended benefit of the proposed plan or project (Wilcox, 2022). A well-framed message includes values like choice, hard work, balance, fairness, and opportunity. Messages should appeal to the values that support or advance the issue, describe how the current situation threatens those values, and offer a solution consistent with the values.

The work of building political will and community support is an iterative and ongoing process. It does not end with the development or commencement of the plan. Sharing success stories in the news media, social media, and local government meetings will help to maintain support. We also acknowledge that the political landscape of even the most rural and smallest of towns does indeed change. Therefore, the work of building political will and community support must also be an enduring commitment to awareness and education to ensure continued support for the community housing journey.

Notes

1 Sweetwater is a pseudonym, See Appendix for more information.
2 Foothills County is a pseudonym. See Appendix for more information.

References

Abt Associates, & NYU Furman Center. (2026). Local Housing Solutions. https://www.localhousingsolutions.org

Adams, B., Welsh Carroll, M., & Gutierrez, N. (2023). Community acceptance of, and opposition to, homeless-serving facilities. *International Journal on Homelessness*, 3(2), 156–183. https://doi.org/10.5206/ijoh.2022.2.14785

Alkon, A. H., & Traugot, M. (2008). Place matters, but how? Rural identity, environmental decision making, and the social construction of place. *City & Community*, 7(2), 97–112. https://doi.org/10.1111/j.1540-6040.2008.00248.x

Ault, M. (2015). *Building support for affordable housing*. National Housing Conference. https://nhc.org/wp-content/uploads/2017/03/Building-Support-for-Affordable-Housing.pdf

Belden, N., Russonello, J., & Vaina, D. (2003). *Valuing housing: Public perceptions of affordable housing in the Chicago region*. Housing Illinois. https://www.housingillinois.org/fullreport.htm

Burningham, K. (2000). Using the language of NIMBY: A topic for research, not an activity for researchers. *Local Environment*, 5(1), 55–67. https://doi.org/10.1080/135498300113264

Catlaw, T. J., & Stout, M. (2016). Governing small-town America today: The promise and dilemma of dense networks. *Public Administration Review*, 76(2), 225–229. https://doi.org/10.1111/puar.12520

Devine-Wright, P. (2009). Rethinking NIMBYism: The role of place attachment and place identity in explaining place-protective action. *Journal of Community & Applied Social Psychology*, 19(6), 426–441. https://doi.org/10.1002/casp.1004

Eranti, V. (2017). Re-visiting NIMBY: From conflicting interests to conflicting valuations. *The Sociological Review*, 65(2), 285–301. https://doi.org/10.1177/0038026116675554

Freudenburg, W. R., & Pastor, S. K. (1992). NIMBYs and LULUs: Stalking the syndromes. *Journal of Social Issues*, 48(4), 39–61. https://doi.org/10.1111/j.1540-4560.1992.tb01944.x

Khaw, K. W., Alnoor, A., Al-Abrrow, H., Tiberius, V., Ganesan, Y., & Atshan, N. A. (2023). Reactions towards organizational change: A systematic literature review. *Current Psychology*, 42(22), 19137–19160. https://doi.org/10.1007/s12144-022-03070-6

Manzo, L. C. (2003). Beyond house and haven: Toward a revisioning of emotional relationships with places. *Journal of Environmental Psychology*, 23(1), 47–61. https://doi.org/10.1016/S0272-4944(02)00074-9

Manzo, L. C., & Perkins, D. D. (2006). Finding common ground: The importance of place attachment to community participation and planning. *Journal of Planning Literature*, 20(4), 335–350. https://doi.org/10.1177/0885412205286160

Marble, W., & Nall, C. (2017). *Beyond "NIMBYism": Why Americans support affordable housing but oppose local housing development*. https://housingforwardva.org/research-tags/nimby/

Oliver, J. E. (with Ha, S. E., & Callen, Z.). (2012). *Local elections and the politics of small-scale democracy* (First edition). Princeton University Press.

Osinubi, A., Skobba, K., Ziebarth, A., & Tinsley, K. (2022). Perceptions and affordable rental housing: A small-town perspective from Georgia. *Housing and Society*, 49(2), 187–208. https://doi.org/10.1080/08882746.2021.1940447

Pardo Del Val, M., & Martínez Fuentes, C. (2003). Resistance to change: A literature review and empirical study. *Management Decision*, 41(2), 148–155. https://doi.org/10.1108/00251740310457597

Post, L. A., Raile, A. N. W., & Raile, E. D. (2010). Defining political will. *Politics & Policy*, 38(4), 653–676. https://doi.org/10.1111/j.1747-1346.2010.00253.x

Poulsen, M., Spiker, M., & Winch, P. (2014). Conceptualizing community buy-in and its application to urban farming. *Journal of Agriculture, Food Systems, and Community Development*, 5(1), 161–178. https://doi.org/10.5304/jafscd.2014.051.014

Proshansky, H. M., Fabian, A. K., & Kaminoff, R. (1983). Place-identity: Physical world socialization of the self. *Journal of Environmental Psychology*, 3(1), 57–83. https://doi.org/10.1016/S0272-4944(83)80021-8

Radosevich, J., & Turner, D. (2024, October 9). *Americans recognize housing affordability crisis, support new policies to fix the market and build more homes* [Center for American Progress]. https://www.americanprogress.org/article/americans-recognize-housing-affordability-crisis-support-new-policies-to-fix-the-market-and-build-more-homes/

Scally, C. P. (2014a). NIMBY: Where, when, and to which developers it happens. *Shelterforce*. https://shelterforce.org/2014/04/01/nimby_where_when_and_to_which_developers_it_happens/

Scally, C. P. (2014b). Who, why, and how communities oppose affordable housing. *Shelterforce*. https://shelterforce.org/2014/04/23/who_why_and_how_communities_oppose_affordable_housing/

Trautman, R. R. (2016). Small-town policy makers. *Public Administration Review*, 76(2), 221–224. https://doi.org/10.1111/puar.12526

Wilcox, M. (2022). *From networking to collaboration, from buy-in to active engagement*. Purdue University – Extension. https://extension.purdue.edu/news/cdext/2022/09/from-networking-to-collaboration-from-buy-in-to-active-engagement.html

9

GETTING TO KNOW YOUR COMMUNITY

With engaged community leaders and a housing team in place and ready to tackle housing challenges, you may feel the momentum (or pressure) to get started. A group of stakeholders in Glenwood, Minnesota, was in this spot. Like many rural communities, their Eureka Moment arrived with the realization that a lack of housing was affecting the local employers and employees. However, the group needed more information about the community and its housing needs before taking any action (Kallevig, n.d.). Working with the University of Minnesota's Center for Small Towns, the group decided on a workforce housing study using a community survey and focus groups (Asche et al., 2016). The housing study engaged a diverse range of community members in the process—people with various roles, experiences, interests, and demographic characteristics. The study confirmed that employees had difficulty finding housing in the city of Glenwood and the county, with renters under the age of 40 facing the most significant housing challenges. The results also highlighted the poor quality of the rental housing options and the gap in homes that

DOI: 10.4324/9781003520450-9

were available, affordable, and in adequate condition for purchase by the local workforce.

The Glenwood, Minnesota case example highlights the importance of collecting data to inform the community housing planning process. Conducting a community housing study can confirm that the original problem is, in fact, the most pressing housing problem. The results may also provide a more nuanced understanding of the problem. Evaluating the results of your housing needs assessment will help create a housing work plan that focuses on and prioritizes the challenges while also identifying resource gaps and strengths.

This chapter offers a process for gathering and collecting data on community demographics, employment, and housing characteristics. The process includes examining the gaps within the community using the 5A framework—access, adequacy, affordability, appropriateness, and availability.

The 5A Framework for Evaluating Community Housing Challenges

To examine the state of housing in a local community, we start by using the 5A framework for assessing community housing challenges. The 5A framework evaluates housing problems regarding accessibility, adequacy, affordability, appropriateness, and availability (Crump, 2003; Green et al., 2000; Ziebarth et al., 2000). This framework provides a way to assess the housing factors that contribute to sufficient housing in a community.

Adequacy—Adequacy refers to the condition of the local housing stock (Crump, 2003; Green et al., 2000; Ziebarth et al., 2000). Adequacy is determined by looking at housing quality issues within occupied housing, including complete and functional plumbing, electrical systems that work throughout the home and are free of exposed wires, and operational heating, ventilation, and air conditioning systems (Eggers & Moumen, 2013). Housing adequacy results from proper home maintenance. Conversely, lack of regular maintenance and repair results in substandard and dilapidated housing.

Affordability—Affordability refers to the alignment between housing costs and household incomes. For the U.S., the standard measure is that households should not have to spend more than 30% of their income on housing costs. The affordability measure is based on the premise that housing is a basic need that consumes a significant amount of a household's budget, yet households have other essential needs that also cost money. When households spend more than 30% of their income on housing, they may not have enough left over to cover other expenses such as food, transportation, and medical expenses. The 30% standard is not a perfect measure, but it is relatively easy to assess and understand using available data. The 30% standard can be applied at a community level to determine how many households are *cost-burdened*, exceeding 30% of their income on housing costs, or expending more than 50% of their income, referred to as *severe housing cost burden*.

Appropriateness—Appropriateness refers to the extent to which the housing in the community matches the needs of current and future residents (Crump, 2003; Ziebarth et al., 2000). This aspect includes the range of ways in which the housing options in the community are suitable when compared to household characteristics. It is essentially a "fit test." Appropriateness also includes options for renting and homeownership as well as variations in home size (square footage and number of bedrooms) relative to household size. An assessment of appropriateness may also include overcrowding among families in the community (Crump, 2003).

Availability—Availability refers to the existing housing stock in the community by structure type (single-family homes, townhouses, apartments, and condos) (Green et al., 2000; Ziebarth et al., 2000). Consideration is also given to whether housing is available for rent or ownership, measured in terms of vacancy rates. It is essential to look at vacancy rates among different types of housing and cost levels because the availability of rental housing and homes for sale often varies by price and affordability levels (Crump, 2003). The availability of subsidized housing (public housing, Section 8, affordable senior housing) is often measured by the length of waiting lists.

Accessibility—Accessibility refers to the extent to which barriers exist limiting entry into housing (Green et al., 2000). Barriers can exist through financial-, public-, and private-sector policies as well as individual and structural mechanisms. Financial barriers exist when there are limited options for financing housing or when the cost of housing is high relative to local incomes. Housing costs are a consistent and often the most significant barrier in a community, which is why this particular financial barrier has its own "A" (affordability). Public policy mechanisms can restrict access to housing through zoning regulations, constraining the types of housing built in the community, or narrowing access to rental housing assistance. Private-sector policy influences can include landlords levying high security deposits and strict requirements for first and last month rent. Tenant screening policies can also restrict access for people with no or poor credit histories or relatively minor criminal histories. Discrimination and racial segregation also create barriers to housing and can limit access to jobs, quality schools, grocery stores, and community amenities.

Community Housing Needs Assessments

In the first year of the Georgia Initiative for Community Housing program, housing teams usually gather and assess data about their community. One of the common approaches is to conduct a comprehensive housing needs assessment (Figure 9.1). Asking and answering questions about the key factors that influence current and future community housing needs can aid in the identification of the community's most pressing gaps and housing challenges. The assessment process typically involves gathering and evaluating information: demographic, economic, and housing data about individuals and households in the community as well as housing stock characteristics. Housing needs assessments may include an inventory of community resources and services and an assessment of exterior housing conditions.

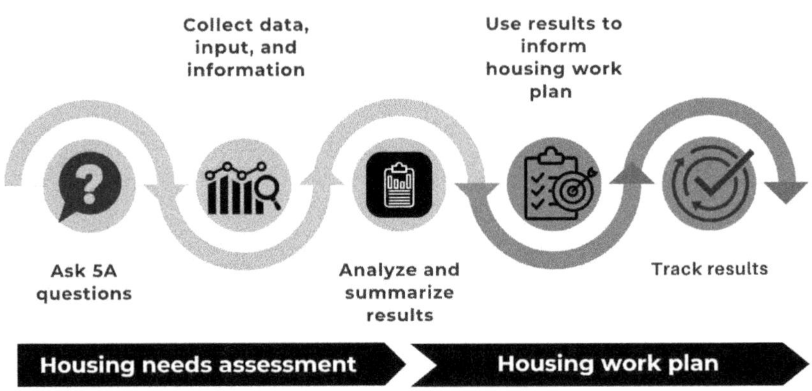

Figure 9.1 Housing needs assessment process.

Source: Authors.

Gathering input from residents and stakeholder groups using surveys, forums, or focus groups is critical to community housing assessments. When finished, a housing needs assessment provides a comprehensive evaluation of housing supply and demand not merely based on data points but also contextualized by detailed input from community residents and stakeholders to identify both current and future housing needs. This information empowers your housing team with the clearest picture possible of the most pressing housing challenges as well as the housing options needed and desired by the community. This information will help your housing team set priorities when developing a work plan.

Begin by Asking Questions

The housing needs assessment process begins with identifying and defining the problem by generating a set of questions you want answered through the assessment. Thinking through these questions will ensure that you are collecting the quantitative and qualitative data needed to understand the community's housing challenges. Use the 5A framework—adequacy, affordability, appropriateness, availability, and accessibility to help your housing team identify areas of focus (Table 9.1).

Gathering Community-Based Data

After considering the 5A questions, the next step is to find the data sources that will provide the answers needed to develop your community's housing plan. In our experience, communities take several different paths at this stage. Some have funds to hire consultants or third-party organizations while others complete the work on their own or with the help of a partner organization, such as a state regional planning representative or a nearby college or university.

The information in this section is designed to walk you through the housing needs assessment process. If your housing team conducts the assessment, whether by choice or necessity, search the internet for resources. There are a number of websites and guides that provide detailed steps in the community housing assessment process. There are also resources on

Table 9.1 5A Questions

Factor	*Questions to Consider*
Adequacy	• How many homes show *physical signs* of: (1) severe disrepair—such as structural damage, unsafe living conditions, inadequate/lack of utilities; or (2) minor disrepair—such as peeling paint, broken fixtures, unsafe steps, or general neglect? • Are unhoused people living in *housing alternatives*: (1) garages, sheds, or vehicles; (2) campgrounds, motels/hotels, and mini-warehouses; or (3) vacant buildings or makeshift campsites? • In areas affected by *natural disasters* (tornadoes, flooding, severe storms, etc.), how many homes still require repairs a year or more after the event—particularly for damage like roof damage, mold, or structural instability?
Affordability	• How do housing *costs compare* to local household *incomes* and typical *wages?* • How many households—by income group—experience *housing cost burden* or *severe housing cost burden?* • Are there housing options for households across the income spectrum, to rent or own, without spending more than 30% of their income—and where are the gaps if not? • How is affordability affecting *local workforce* recruitment and retention? Are essential workers (public safety, health care, and teaching staff) and young adults able to afford to live in or return to the community?
Appropriateness	• What is the *mix of housing types and sizes* to meet the needs of different household compositions—including one-person households, families with children, and those seeking to upsize or downsize? • Is there *suitable housing* for various preferences and needs, including first-time buyers, low-maintenance living, congregate arrangements, and barrier-free housing for elders aging in place or people with disabilities? • Are there reports from *housing misalignment* causing distressed living conditions, such as families living in overcrowded homes or excessive community due to a lack of appropriate housing options locally?

Table 9.1 (Continued)

Factor	*Questions to Consider*
Availability	• What is the *composition of the housing stock*—percentage of single-family, townhouses, apartments/lofts, missing middle options (duplexes, triplexes, quadplexes), accessory dwelling units (ADUs), and mobile/manufactured homes—and how does this align with local housing needs? • How many housing units are *available* (sale or lease) and at what *cost* (price points or rental rates) presently? What are the *residential vacancy rates* for both owner-occupied and rental properties? • Is there *overwhelming unmet demand* like a large applicant pool or long waiting list for affordable housing or subsidized (public housing/private Section 8) housing?
Accessibility	• Do local *land use regulations* (plans, subdivisions, zoning) support or restrict development of diverse housing types? If there are incentivized alternative regulations, such as planned developments, are they utilized—why or why not? • Are *financial barriers*—credit score requirements, limited access to mortgage financing, or lack of savings—keeping prospective renters or buyers from securing housing? • Do other *housing hurdles*, such as rental application policies, background checks, or access to services (transportation, groceries, schools) vary across different groups—potentially creating unequal barriers to housing?

Source: Authors, adapted from Crump (2003), Green et al. (2000), and Ziebarth et al. (2000).

specific data collection tools and methods. Identify people and organizations with housing and community development expertise. We have frequently provided guidance and student support to help with data collection and analysis for communities in the Georgia Initiative for Community Housing program.

Community housing needs assessments take time and require you to either find outside assistance or develop expertise. Paying someone else to complete all or part of your community housing assessment can save you time and provide the credibility of a third-party expert. Ensure you select a person or organization with experience as well as strong interpersonal and communication skills. You want someone who will answer your questions, listen to your concerns, and keep the housing team engaged throughout the process.

You will need both primary and secondary data to answer your questions. Primary data is collected by your housing team, a consultant, or community volunteers for a specific purpose. Examples include community surveys, focus groups, community input sessions, and windshield surveys. Secondary data is data collected by another person or organization for some other purpose but is helpful in answering your questions. U.S. Census data, county tax assessor data, and other public and proprietary data are all secondary data. We have identified various data sources and data collection methods commonly employed in developing a community housing needs assessment. Keep in mind that these are options, not requirements. Pick data sources that are feasible and will best help your housing team understand the needs of your community.

Gathering Data about the Community and Housing

U.S. Census Data

Questions about community demographic, economic, and housing characteristics can usually be answered with data from the U.S. Census. American Community Survey (ACS) five-year estimate data can show trends over time as well as a snapshot from recent years. The data provides important statistics about who lives in the community, including a breakdown by age groups, household income, and the percentage of families living below the poverty level, homeownership rates, and the prevalence of housing cost burden. This data also provides a breakdown of the housing stock by the type of housing and the age of the community's housing stock. Together, these measures can provide insight into current gaps in housing as well as future housing needs.

You can gather data directly from the U.S. Census website or use free versions of tools like Social Explorer and PolicyMap. Local Housing Solutions offers a free housing needs assessment tool that will create a report for any city, county, or metro area in the U.S. While American Community Survey data offers valuable data for a community housing needs assessment, it has some limitations for smaller communities. The American Community Survey is a national survey that uses *representative sampling* to create estimates for Census tracts, cities, counties, states, and other geographies. The smaller populations of small towns and rural counties mean that measures often have large margins of error, which can render the data less accurate (Scally et al., 2020). However, it is often the only data source for key demographic and economic measures. If you use ACS data, remember that five-year estimates are more accurate, even though they may include a range of years that may make the data seem less relevant than one-year estimates.

Tax Assessor Data

County tax assessor data can also be a good source of local data for understanding housing characteristics. Tax assessor data allows for an analysis of various housing attributes, such as square footage, number of bedrooms, age, market value, and occupancy status of residential units by city or county and areas within a city or county. Several communities in the Georgia Initiative for Community Housing have used this data to calculate the homeownership/renter rates by comparing the address of the property owner to the address where tax notices are sent. Use of parcel data takes time. Someone with spreadsheet skills will need to sort and analyze your measures of interest. However, it may be worth the effort to glean insights using data that is collected at the local level.

Planning Data and Spatial Tools

Local governments maintain data that can enhance the understanding of your community's housing stock. For instance, local planning departments generally issue and track permits, which may reveal building trends as well as market preferences regarding new homes, additions, and renovations. Beyond how housing is being expanded and updated, construction data can be indicative of housing preferences or even a unique local challenge, such as a paucity of homebuilders. Code enforcement offices retain records regarding minimum maintenance complaints, compliance activity, and unfit buildings, which is useful for questions about housing adequacy. Similarly, some city and county utility departments may be good resources regarding housing occupancy, tenure, and stressors, where active utility accounts are tracked, lease information is required for connection, and disconnects often occur. These local data sources, while sometimes requiring more effort to access and analyze, can provide a more granular and timely picture of development patterns and housing conditions than secondary datasets alone. Local planning data can assist teams in building a more comprehensive, locally grounded housing needs assessment.

Utilizing common planning tools, such as Geographic Information Systems (GIS), enables communities to visualize, analyze, and interpret data spatially. A map illustrating where new housing starts are occurring and where rehabilitation and additions are primarily focused is extremely informative as to which neighborhoods are nascent, maturing, or declining. This powerful tool can be used to analyze land use and zoning implications, identify concentrations of substandard housing, depict the property valuation spectrum, and locate potential infill opportunities. GIS integrates various data layers—such as parcel boundaries, building footprints, demographic data, as well as infrastructure networks—into a single interactive resource. This empowers planners and housing teams to make data-informed decisions, such as identifying areas suitable for new development, targeting neighborhoods for intervention, or evaluating the impact of policy changes. Local governments may have internal GIS services or depend upon regional planning agencies to manage and update their data. Used in combination with housing conditions surveys and collected input, GIS can be an essential tool for visual storytelling, strategic planning, and work plan development.

Housing Assessment Surveys

Housing assessment surveys, sometimes referred to as windshield surveys or housing conditions surveys, involve field evaluations of residential buildings (houses, duplexes, and apartments) and lot conditions. While the primary focus is on homes, surveys may also include vacant lots and commercial properties. Trained volunteers use paper or digital surveys to gather data on home exteriors, making observations from streets or sidewalks. This process provides a snapshot of current housing conditions, enabling the identification of substandard housing. Surveys may be conducted by individuals or teams over several weeks or months, depending on the target area. Volunteers can include community members, city staff, and students—all valuable contributors (Figure 9.2).

Windshield survey data provides important insights about exterior housing conditions, which can be helpful before developing housing goals and strategies. The data provides a starting point to identify substandard and

Figure 9.2 Volunteers conducting a housing assessment survey.

Photo credit: Authors.

dilapidated housing within the community. This information helps target areas of need for current and future projects (Housing and Demographic Research Center, n.d.).

Other Sources of Local Data

Some organizations may also have local data that is more current and specific than Census data (Abt Associates and NYU Furman Center, 2026). For example, a Habitat for Humanity affiliate offers insightful demand data by sharing that though they could only select one homebuyer, 24 households qualified for the newest house they are building. Local nonprofit organizations and school districts may also possess data contributing to your understanding of local housing needs. Realtors and appraisers may have data on the housing market, including recent transactions' home sales, available inventory, turnover rates, list and sales prices, etc. (Ziebarth et al., 2000).

Gathering Data from the Community

Collecting input from residents and other stakeholder groups is an integral part of the community housing assessment process. Gathering data from local stakeholders provides timely information that can help pinpoint specific housing challenges and prioritize your housing work plan strategies. While Census data can yield insight into demographic, economic, and housing characteristics, it does not provide the understanding offered by collecting information from community members. Gathering the perspectives of stakeholder groups through interviews and focus groups can give context to any statistics you have collected.

There are several ways to gather input from your local community. Surveys, community forums, individual and focus group interviews are common methods. Below is a description of each method, what is involved, and the pros and cons.

Surveys

Community-based surveys use web-based or paper questionnaires to gather feedback, opinions, and information from individuals within a community. Surveys can focus on input from specific groups within the community, such as residents, community leaders, and local employers, or can be developed in a way that allows for input from a variety of stakeholders. Community-based surveys about housing are relatively common, making it easy to generate ideas from examples available online. Surveys offer several benefits. With sufficient promotion and distribution, they can garner input from many people in a relatively short timeframe. Surveys can be a relatively low-cost way to gather information. Web-based survey tools often have free or low-cost subscription rates, are easy to use, and have tools that make it easier to analyze results. However, internet surveys can be less accessible for some community members and may result in "ballot box stuffing" (Vincent II, 2014). Paper surveys can be mailed directly to community members, increasing accessibility and reducing the ballot stuffing issue. Print surveys require significant labor for data entry and analysis, and combined with printing and mailing, contribute to higher costs than web-based surveys. If you are considering conducting a survey, we recommend you review one of the many resources available online (See Harrison et al., 2021; University of Kansas Center for Community Health and Development, 2025). Partnering with a class at a community college or university in your region or state is also a good way to obtain no- or low-cost assistance with a survey project.

Individual and Group Interviews

While the formats have some differences, individual and group interviews share the feature of posing questions to gather deep insights and perspectives on a topic of interest. Individual interviews are one-on-one conversations that are about 30–60 minutes in length using a structured set of open-ended questions. Group interviews, also called focus groups, are conducted using a facilitator who asks a structured set of questions over a 60–90-minute interview. Groups include about 5–8 people. At the beginning of the interview, the facilitator discusses the purpose, meeting agenda, and ground rules. Then, the facilitator begins asking questions, giving everyone in the group a chance to respond before opening the question up for discussion. It is common to conduct several focus groups on a given topic. There are pros and cons to using interviews in general and individual versus focus groups. An advantage of both formats is that you can gather detailed feedback from different perspectives on community housing needs. For example, interviews with people in the community who hear from or help others find housing can provide information on varying experiences—from those who work with residents experiencing housing insecurity to homeowners looking to upgrade or downsize. Realtors, appraisers, and mortgage lenders can help you understand barriers to homeownership and gaps in the housing for first-time homebuyers and those looking to upgrade or downsize. A disadvantage of using interviews is that you hear from a limited number of community members. This can result in a narrower input that overlooks crucial information about housing issues affecting the community. However, with proper planning and input, interviews can garner multiple perspectives and uncover various housing issues.

There are a few differences between individual and focus group interview formats. Focus groups are an efficient way to gather feedback from one or more stakeholder groups. They are less time-intensive, which means you can gather in-depth feedback from many people in a relatively short time frame. Interviews require more time because you are collecting feedback from one person at a time. This requires time to schedule and conduct the interviews, which can add up if you need to talk with 10 or more people. Individual interviews allow for private and longer, more detailed responses than focus groups. Focus groups are conducted with 6–8 people at a time, which means each person will have a few minutes to respond to each question. Both interview formats require some time afterward to review notes or transcripts for patterns of responses. Organizing this information into findings for your community housing assessment is helpful.

Community Meetings

Community meetings, also called public forums or community input sessions, are structured gatherings open to all community members. They are designed to bring together community members to discuss and identify housing issues. Community meetings offer the advantage of gathering input from a large and diverse group. They can be more challenging to manage due to the larger number of participants and the potential for divisive conversation.

Community meetings work best when they are well-publicized, held in convenient public locations, and attended by a wide range of people in the community (University of Kansas Center for Community Health and Development, 2025). Like focus groups, community forums use a facilitator who manages the session and asks structured questions to prompt discussion. During the community meeting, responses are documented, typically on easel paper or sticky notes, and themes are summarized at the end of the meeting. Community spaces that allow for seating by tables provide the opportunity for small group discussion with a leader at each table are ideal. Avoid auditorium seating, which can limit the discussion to a few voices.

The Community Tool Box (University of Kansas, 2025) provides detailed steps, checklists, and questions to consider that can easily be adapted to focus on housing issues in the community.

Putting It All Together: Community Data Collection Results

You have asked the questions, collected the data, and examined your results. Now what do you do? In the next chapter, we will cover how you will use the information from your assessment to develop a housing work plan. But before you start planning, you may want to share your findings in a report or presentation. Consider including the following information:

- The purpose of your project and what you hoped to learn
- A summary of the data used or collected
- Insights learned from data collected *about* the community (demographic, economic, and housing data)
- Insights from data gathered *from* the community (survey results, interviews, and focus group findings)
- Summarize overall findings and identify housing gaps and barriers
- Recommendations/strategies (if available, you can also develop these in the planning process).

Compiling the information into a comprehensive report or presentation will allow you to easily share insights with stakeholders such as elected officials, community organizations, and residents. The goal is to use the findings to inform decision-making, prioritize housing needs, and develop actionable strategies for addressing identified challenges. We will cover these steps in the next chapter on planning for community housing.

References

Abt Associates & NYU Furman Center. (2026). Using local housing data. Housing Solutions Lab. https://www.localhousingsolutions.org/analyze/using-local-housing-data/

Asche, K., Pesch, R., & Cook, B. (2016). *Workforce housing in Pope County*. Center for Small Towns, University of Minnesota.

Crump, J. (2003). *A guide to neighborhood housing assessment: A student workbook*. University of Minnesota. https://conservancy.umn.edu/server/api/core/bitstreams/8043ff4e-befc-4cff-9d32-c7f5b5b1d530/content

Eggers, F., & Moumen, F. (2013). *American housing survey: Housing adequacy and quality as measured by the AHS* (SSRN Scholarly Paper No. 2284174). https://doi.org/10.2139/ssrn.2284174

Green, G. P., Haines, A., & Halebsky, S. (2000). *Building our future: A guide to community visioning* (Cooperative Extension No. G3708). University of Wisconsin, Madison. https://learningstore.extension.wisc.edu/products/building-our-future-a-guide-to-community-visioning-p231

Harrison, E., Mizota, M., Daly, H., & Falkenburger, E. (2021). *Community-Engaged surveys: From research design to analysis and dissemination*. Urban Institute. https://www.urban.org/sites/default/files/publication/104934/community-engaged-surveys-from-research-design-to-analysis-and-dissemination_0.pdf

Housing and Demographic Research Center. (n.d.). *Housing assessment guide*. University of Georgia. https://www.fcs.uga.edu/docs/HDRC_HousingAssessmentGuide.pdf

Kallevig, C. (n.d.). *Glenwood's housing study results* (No. 11) [Broadcast]. https://extension.umn.edu/vital-connections-air/episode-11-glenwoods-housing-study-results

Scally, C., Burnstein, E., Gerken, M., & Immonen, E. (2020). *In search of "good" rural data*. Urban Institute. https://www.urban.org/sites/default/files/publication/102134/in-search-of-good-rural-data.pdf

University of Kansas Center for Community Health and Development. (2025). *Community tool box*. https://ctb.ku.edu/en/table-of-contents/assessment/assessing-community-needs-and-resources/conduct-surveys/main

Vincent II, J. W. (2014). Community development assessments. In R. Phillips (Ed.), *An introduction to community development* (pp. 133–153). Routledge.

Ziebarth, A., Brown, K., & Elgalatian, P. (2000). *Community housing development: Building a brighter future*. University of Illinois Extension Service.

10

PLANNING FOR COMMUNITY HOUSING

Over the past several years, we have noted a common theme echoed in meetings about housing in rural communities—*We need more housing and we need it now!* As professionals who spend too many hours every week studying and working on rural- and small-town housing problems, we get it. There is no need to convince us. We understand the situation.

Unfortunately, housing takes time. Housing, understood as community infrastructure, requires deliberate and strategic effort to change, particularly given that most housing teams do not actually construct the infrastructure. Teams coax it into the desired shape. A long-time facilitator working with the Georgia Initiative for Community Housing (GICH) program once summarized this hard truth in one sentence—*The housing problems in your community developed over decades, so they will not be fixed overnight.* The upside of this reality may be an easing of the unfair, overwhelming weight of believing it is possible to solve your community's housing crisis by next year.

DOI: 10.4324/9781003520450-10

Housing Work Plans: A Roadmap for the Community Housing Journey

The community housing approach is more of a marathon than a sprint. Most aptly, it may be described as a journey. Most small towns lack the capacity or partnerships necessary to achieve significant housing gains in the short term. For those who do, housing development still takes time. It may take years of hard work before you make a major dent in your community's housing needs. However, with a housing work plan in place, you will see progress by tackling smaller initiatives or incremental objectives that, over time, add up to significant change. Along the way, your housing team can develop knowledge and skills, as well as build essential partnerships, to help you achieve your long-term housing goals.

A housing work plan draws a roadmap to obtainable housing outcomes—the change you desire. To extend the metaphor, the work plan is not only a statement of your destination. It also steers the course forward, ensuring that both your team and your community are aware of the itinerary. Imagine it is a bus trip. Ideally, your housing plan should identify the trip details that you and your passengers need to know: where you are going, why you are going there, and what you hope to see when you arrive. If the destination is a long way away, can you break up the trip to make it doable? How long is the trip expected to take? Who will drive, and who will you take along with you? How much will the trip cost, and how much travel money will be needed? Finally, what signs indicate your arrival?

Successful work plans start with clear and defined goals (aspirations, outcomes, destinations). Some goals, like some trips, are quick. Others may need to be broken into individual segments or work items, also referred to as action items, tasks, or activities. A work item might achieve the goal, or it may be one of several necessary to meet the goal. The work plan also provides an estimated timeframe, which can be stated as a deadline, a range of time, or even more categorically as short-term, mid-term, and long-term. The strongest work plans assign and disperse responsibility as well as identify likely partnerships. From practical experience, we know that work plans are likely to fall short of aspirations when they do not identify who is accountable for each item or when every item is assigned to the team leader or staff. Similarly, no work items should be included without at least contemplation of probable costs and required resources. This item includes identifying prospective funding sources if the costs of work items are significant.

Often undervalued, a work plan section devoted to project status, including refinements, milestones, or achievements, is essential. Accountability and transparency are not just buzzwords; they are common expectations in the community today. The work plan status section is necessary for keeping the whole housing team informed when work items are well-delegated and communicated succinctly and accurately to officials and the public. Communicating the work plan status also helps keep the housing team on task when turnover occurs among team leaders and members. Work plan updates may also include performance measures or key performance indicators (e.g., the number of homes repaired, total attendance at a housing credit workshop, or the number of training hours earned by housing team members). All of these work plan elements come together so that not only can someone read the roadmap, but they can also see how far you have traveled.

Mapping the Route: Laying the Groundwork for Planning

The planning process begins with initial activities that provide the foundation for developing your housing team's work plan. As you start these activities, it is helpful to identify a facilitator to guide the discussion. Your facilitator can be a member of your team or someone in the community who is good at listening and guiding group conversations.

Housing Team SWOT Analysis

Figuring out how and where to start with your housing work plan can be daunting. Starting with a relatively easy task can make the process of getting started easier. Communities participating in the GICH program typically begin their planning process by conducting a SWOT analysis. SWOT analysis, short for **S**trengths, **W**eaknesses, **O**pportunities, and **T**hreats, guides brainstorming and strategic discussions about housing and community development (Abt Associates, 2016). By completing a SWOT analysis, you gain an understanding of your housing team's collective assets and resources, as well as any gaps and potential barriers. Results inform the housing planning process by helping your team to identify clear objectives based on a comprehensive understanding of available capacity and capabilities (U.S. Economic Development Administration, 2025). Let's look at the SWOT elements as they apply to housing work plan development.

Strengths and Weaknesses

Your housing team's strengths are its positive qualities, experiences, and resources. Strengths can include intangible attributes (such as enthusiasm, commitment, influence, experience, and trust among team members) and tangible assets (such as funding, available land, and dedicated staff time). Weaknesses represent the limitations facing your housing team. Examples of weaknesses include a lack of housing expertise, limited funding, and outdated housing regulations. Include strengths and weaknesses specific to housing, as well as attributes of the housing team and community.

Opportunities and Threats

Opportunities are external factors that offer favorable conditions to support your work or position your housing team for success, such as a strong local economy, access to university resources and assistance, and quality infrastructure. Threats are factors that pose obstacles to your work, yet are outside the control of your housing team. Common threats to community housing include a weak local or regional economy, national economic downturns, a lack of a construction/development workforce or businesses, and policy changes that result in the loss of program funding, financial incentives, or increased regulations.

The SWOT Discussion

You may want team members to complete the SWOT questions independently before the group discussion to ensure everyone has had time to think about the questions. When meeting as a group, appoint a facilitator to guide the conversation. Having someone write down ideas on easel paper or a whiteboard will help everyone in the group keep track of the items discussed. Consider using the questions in Table 10.1 to guide your discussion. Numerous online resources can also assist you in planning and implementing a SWOT analysis.

Table 10.1 SWOT Discussion Questions

Strengths	*Weaknesses*
Team Attributes	
• What knowledge or connections does your team bring to the table? • What resources—such as funding, partnerships, or community support—are available to your team right now? • Are there other assets or capabilities in your team or community to help?	• What expertise or skills does your team need to address housing issues? • What critical resources—such as connections, investment, and collaborations—are currently missing? • Are there other internal weaknesses that were not identified above?
Housing/Housing-Related Attributes	
• What aspects of housing are working well or meeting needs effectively? • What groups in the community have stable housing—secure and sufficient? • Where and when does the community currently show support or discuss housing?	• What are the most pressing housing issues—think about the 5As (Chapter 9)? • Where are those challenges most visible or concentrated? For whom? • How does the community currently respond to housing concerns?
Opportunities • What current trends or external forces—economic shifts, demographic changes, or political change—could support housing improvements? • Is there upcoming legislation that might benefit your housing efforts? • Who can you work with to advance housing solutions? Are there existing collaborations you can strengthen or new ones that can expand impact? • What storytelling or communications activities could build public support for housing initiatives?	**Threats** • What external forces or factors—such as market volatility, climate risks, or materials/labor—are impacting local housing but are outside your control? • What existing policies, regulations, or political dynamics could limit or halt progress on housing initiatives? • Are there competing community priorities diverting attention or resources away from housing? • What groups or parts of your community will actively oppose housing options?

Table 10.1 (Continued)

Strengths	*Weaknesses*
• What funding sources—grants, public-private partnerships, or philanthropic investments—are currently accessible or pending for housing-related work? • What innovations or technologies might improve housing outcomes?	• Are there other external limitations—such as public perception, legal challenges, or infrastructure gaps? • Is there a lack of reliable data or research that makes it harder to advocate for housing solutions?

Source: Authors; Abt Associates, 2016.

At the end of the SWOT analysis process, summarize the key findings in each category. These findings will provide the starting point for developing your housing work plan. The results of your SWOT analysis will inform the strategic priorities and action items in your housing work plan (U.S. Economic Development Administration, 2025).

Housing Team Visioning Process

With your SWOT analysis complete, you now have insights about both your housing team and your community. The next step, housing team visioning, creates a shared picture of what you want your community to look like or the desired impacts resulting from your hard work. Okubo (2009, p. 77) highlights the importance of visioning in achieving goals.

> Some communities allow the future to happen to them. Thriving communities recognize that the future is something they can create. These communities take the time to produce a shared vision of the future they desire and employ a process that helps them achieve their goals. Achieving the desired future is hard work. Yet successful communities understand that the things they dream about will only come true through great effort, determination, and teamwork.

Your team's visioning work may include some preliminary discussion of potential goals or incremental steps, to briefly "test fit" or check feasibility, timing, or both. The purpose of this discussion is not to limit larger aspirations; instead, it can help tailor your visioning process so that it aligns with your community's character, needs, and preferences. Above all else, visioning is a collaborative process to identify your community's future through member engagement and long-term thinking. Having a clear vision for your community's future housing will provide a guiding north star for your planning efforts.

When undertaking housing team visioning and plan development, we propose a relatively straightforward process that can be completed during a two-hour meeting. Have your appointed facilitator guide the discussion. Make sure that someone in the group is taking notes.

The visioning process is guided by three overarching questions: What is? What if? What next? (Hopkins et al., 2024). The question of "What is?" involves taking stock of the current situation. What is and is not working? What needs to be changed? Okubo (2009) describes this step as a community scan. If you have conducted a housing needs assessment and completed a SWOT analysis, your group has already considered "What is?" Review the findings of your previous work and summarize the current housing situation in the community. It may be helpful to organize your findings using the 5A of housing covered in Chapter 9.

After completing the community scan, your housing team will move to the "What if?" stage, exploring your housing team's imagined future. When conducting a community visioning session, Green et al. (2000, pp. 5–3) recommend beginning with an exercise that prompts group members to think about the future: *It is 20 years in the future. You have successfully created the desired housing stock in the community. Describe it.* This exercise, along with the questions below, helps guide the "What if?" part of the visioning process.

1 *Preserving what matters.* What types of housing do you believe are important to preserve? Are there specific neighborhoods or areas you feel should be protected or maintained?
2 *Improving existing homes and areas.* Which housing needs improvement in the community? Are there particular neighborhoods or locations that deserve focused attention?
3 *Imagining new housing options.* What kinds of new housing would you like to see added to the community? Are there existing buildings, lots, or areas that could be repurposed or developed for new housing?

4 *Looking ahead.* What do you want the residential community to look like in 20 years? How does your vision align with what others might want for the community? How can preserving or improving current housing and neighborhoods help realize your long-term vision for the community? In what ways does new housing contribute to achieving your future vision for the community

By the end of your "What if" discussion, your group will likely have many ideas about your community's housing and neighborhoods. Close out this process by working as a group to organize your discussion results into themes (Hopkins et al., 2024). Keeping the themes specific enough to provide direction and broad enough to allow for multiple strategies when used in a housing work plan is helpful.

The final step, "What Next?," aims to lead your group from its envisioned future to reality by identifying goals and action steps. Have someone in your group write the final list of themes generated from the "What if?" discussion on one or more large sheets of easel paper. Give each person in the group three to five dot stickers to place next to the items they believe should be priorities for the team. Team members can apply more than one of their allotted dots if an item is a high priority. Once everyone is finished, review the themes identified as the highest-priority items (Hopkins et al., 2024). Do not be afraid to identify and prioritize the top three to five items so that the team can engage in focused work. Remember that no team has enough resources or support to do everything at once. Use a side sheet of paper as a "parking lot" to retain great ideas for future work.

Developing goals and actionable steps is a direct product of the visioning process. The themes from your visioning exercise will serve as the basis for framing and organizing your goals for the plan. For example, a housing team might group its themes as follows: housing stabilization efforts, resident engagement activities, and new housing options. Perhaps another community is solely focused on obtaining new housing units, so their themes might be grouped as multifamily funding sources, land use policy updates, and education on missing middle housing. This effort also proves useful in future steps because thematic grouping of goals can telegraph not only how you might organize your team's work but also the need for working task groups or committees. Note that goals grouped together often rely on the same data sets, similar funding sources, and even the same networks or partnerships.

The next step in this process helps identify work items that require action. Have housing team members identify two or three projects or activities on notecards or sticky notes that would help to address or advance each high-priority theme. Gather and organize the suggested actions and activities by thematic area. These proposed activities will provide a good starting point for developing your housing work plan.

Developing a Housing Work Plan

A housing work plan is both a document (the plan) and a process (actions). The plan is the document that itemizes, prioritizes, and tracks your work. Adaptations are made as objectives are met, new information is acquired, and capacity building is initiated. Actions are the *process* of the community housing approach—the dynamic, strategic, capacity-building activities. It is the "doing" part of the community housing work plan. While the plan charts the path and measures progress, most community housing work is action-oriented in nature (Table 10.2).

From the Plan to Action

How do you move from the plan to action? What is the best way to get started? How do you know where to begin? Before we dig into work plan strategies, we offer a few tips to keep in mind.

Table 10.2 Community Housing Work Plan and Actions

The Plan	*Actions*
Agreed upon housing team goals List of work items/action items Estimated timeframes for completing work Team member roles and responsibilities Estimated costs, if any Potential sources of funding Trackable measures of completed work, with interim progress/status	SWOT analysis and visioning Housing challenges to address, with initial focus areas or priorities Identification of resources and barriers Community-based activities to build trust Gathering information Building partnerships Acquiring resources

Source: Authors.

Figure 10.1 Housing team planning session.

Photo credit: Cal Powell, University of Georgia College of Family and Consumer Sciences.

- *No plan is one-size-fits-all. Every community housing plan will look different.* The common thread among the work plans of GICH communities is that they are all different. Use the information provided to generate ideas for your own community. While you may want to borrow ideas and strategies from other communities, your housing work plan will be unique to your community's specific needs, resources, and dynamics.
- *Don't spend too much time focusing on the perfect plan.* The saying "perfect is the enemy of good" applies to housing work plans. Getting started can be daunting, and it may be tempting to linger by spending a lot of time on the plan without taking action. Spend a meeting or two identifying activities that align with your goals. Get your initial strategy on paper and then get started.
- *Plan for early wins.* Changes in housing can take a long time, but that does not mean you need to wait years to see results. The community housing approach is built on progress made one step at a time. Consider the actions that your housing team can take within the first three to six months, particularly those that are publicly visible. Organizing a community clean-up day, taking the housing team on a tour of aspirational

housing developments in a peer community (and publicizing it), and launching a public awareness campaign to highlight the goals and work of your community housing team are all short-term activities that can generate momentum, build relationships, and foster awareness of your action within the community.

Housing Work Plan Formats

The community housing work plan used in the GICH program is based on an action plan format. Action plans outline how a group or organization will achieve its goals by providing specific steps and details on when and how each step will be carried out (Center for Community Health and Development, 2025; Green et al., 2000). Thus, a community housing work plan is a type of action plan. Action plan formats vary, and numerous templates are available online. However, they typically include the following elements:

- Priority areas and goals
- Strategies and actions
- Team members responsible for actions
- Activity timeframe
- Resources needed
- Action step progress.

Housing work plans are simple documents. Most GICH communities use Word or Excel documents for their community housing work plans. This information may be a relief if you had imagined housing work plans as highly crafted, well-designed reports with extensive text. Effective housing work plans meet the 3C's of action plans—clear, complete, and current (Center for Community Health and Development, 2025). They can be informal as long as they include the relevant details and are clear and complete enough that you and your team members can interpret the content at next month's meeting. If you have ever looked at the to-do list you wrote three days earlier, saw "call Joe" on the list, and wondered who Joe is and why you needed to call him, you understand why clear information matters. Using short phrases is fine as long as they have the relevant details.

Priorities and SMART Goals

After completing the visioning process, your team will have identified its priority areas. Your list might include some items common among rural and small towns across the U.S. Your community may need more affordable rental housing for the local workforce, improvements in your existing rental housing, and/or an increase in the availability of starter homes or mid-priced homes for sale. The visioning process may have identified a need to build public awareness about the community's housing situation or to conduct a housing needs assessment as priorities. Your housing work plan states these priorities as goals or objectives. Goals signal your housing team's priorities and provide markers of progress. Goals should be "SMART"—specific, measurable, attainable, relevant, and time-bound. Specific and measurable, meaning they should be phrased in a clear way, with enough details to provide planning direction, and quantifiable so that you know when you have succeeded in achieving them. Ideally, your housing work plan will include short-term (less than one year), mid-range (one to three years), and long-term goals (five years or more). Starting with attainable goals is fundamental to the success of the community housing approach. Short-term goals often include those more manageable tasks that can provide early wins. They are the achievable, low-hanging fruit that allow you to get started quickly, show results early in the process, and build momentum. Tackling significant housing challenges takes time. Big wins are the cumulative result of many smaller actions.

Strategies and Actions

Strategies and actions refer to the specific approach, projects, activities, and tasks that lead to milestone accomplishments. After identifying goals, your team will compile a list of projects, activities, and tasks that will help you accomplish these goals. Each goal typically involves several activities. For example, if increasing your team's housing knowledge is a goal, the actions listed should be explicitly related to this goal. Activities to address this goal might include: designated housing team sessions to review and discuss the housing information contained in the city's comprehensive plan, a presentation about existing municipal codes and code enforcement, and scheduling a speaker from the housing finance agency to cover financial tools and resources related to housing.

Task Responsibilities

Assigning each action step to one or more housing team members will provide accountability and help ensure that everyone has something to do. Noting who is responsible for each item will make tracking progress easier if you know who oversees each activity. If you are using small task groups of two or three people, ensure that one person is assigned to lead to reduce confusion, conflict, or deflection of responsibility. And encourage all to avoid being the weak link on the school project—we've all been there.

Resources Needed

Resources can include human capital resources (skills and expertise), physical resources (meeting space, land for development), social capital (partners, peer communities, housing team networks), and financial capital (cash on hand, grants, loans). Listing the resources required for each action item helps clarify what is needed to complete the task and sets realistic timeline expectations. For example, if an action item involves securing grant funding, the timeline must account for the application and approval process.

Action Step Status

Keep track of the progress on the items listed in your plan regularly. This step will help your team see the progress you have made, as well as identify any roadblocks that are hindering your efforts. Periodically review your overall progress and accomplishments.

Common Pitfalls to Avoid

A good plan but no follow-through. Your housing team follows all the steps—a SWOT analysis, visioning, goal setting—and you put together a solid work plan. Everyone has an assignment. Two or three months pass, and no one has made any progress. Action has stalled. A few ways to avoid this situation or get back on track after a team has lost momentum include: (1) make sure that everyone is accountable for reporting progress at meetings, (2) check in and provide support and encouragement to team members who are struggling, and (3) regularly (and publicly) celebrating accomplishments—both big and small (Center for Community Health and Development, 2025).

ITEM NO.	ITEM Short Title | Brief Description	Schedule 22/23	23/24	24/25	25/26	26/27	Responsible Party	Estimated Cost	$$$ Source	Progress Measures & Comments
H-22-1	**Housing Assessment**| Conduct a housing inventory and perform windshield survey of housing conditions	X					**Lead: Member #1** Team & Volunteers	$500 Volunteer Time	City Budget - General Fund	**COMPLETED.** Used University Outreach program to assist with data collection; used a consultant to train team members and volunteers; survey conducted over three-month period.
H-22-2	**Educational Workshops**| Host a series of one-hour meetings to inform decision-makers (e.g., housing assessment, local housing policy/processes, existing housing resources, housing funding sources, etc.)	X	X				**Lead: Team Chair** Planning Staff	$0 Volunteer & Staff Time	N/A Use Library Space	**COMPLETED.** Held 6 work sessions – 1 per month; 45-minute presentation/15 minute discussion; invited elected officials and public for presentational; invited relevant resources and partners (e.g., Habitat) to present.
H-22-3	**Neighborhood Outreach**| Select one program to improve immediate residential conditions.		X	X	X		**Lead: Member #2** County Sheriff	$0 Volunteer Time	N/A Free County Service	**IN PROGRESS.** To improve home and neighborhood safety, address signs are being added. Team collects homeowner addresses, submits for free signs, and delivers them for installation. Progress at 65% coverage.
H-22-4	**Neighborhood Events**| Host one event per year to engage a distressed neighborhood and build community support.	X	X	X	X	X	**Lead: Member #2** Planning Staff	$250 Budget	Partner In-Kind	**ONGOING.** YR1: Neighborhood Cleanup (both spring and fall); YR 2: Public Safety Day (partnered with emergency responders); YR 3: planning in progress...
H-23-1	**Housing Rehabilitation: Phase I**| Pursue housing rehabilitation funds to stabilize homes (8-10) in primary target area.		X	X	X	X	**Lead: Member #1** Consultant	$1,000 $15,000 Admin Fees	City Budget - General Fund Donation	**PENDING.** Requested city funds for consultant to write grant; not funded. Repeated request next year; funded. Consultant completed grant application and submitted (Notice in Oct).
H-23-2	**Senior Housing Complex**| Facilitate one (1) affordable senior-housing complex utilizing tax incentive programs (LIHTC)		X	X	X	X	**Lead: Member #3** Team Members	Time & Travel TBD	Federal Housing Program	**NOT STARTED.** Team visiting communities with Low-Income Housing Tax Credit (LIHTC) projects and researching their developers

Figure 10.2 Example housing work plan.

Source: Authors.

Actions without a sufficiently developed foundation. In a previous chapter, we described one housing team's experience with community opposition to a proposed affordable housing development. The example highlights the challenges of moving ahead with action plan items without completing the groundwork. Other examples of this include spending time and possibly money applying for funding without thoroughly researching the program, and applying for and receiving funding without the capacity to complete the project. If your team is unprepared to address a housing plan goal, proceed slowly and start with small steps.

Inclusion of only long-term goals. Without short and mid-range goals, housing teams lose momentum, support, and trust while waiting for something big to happen. The team may also lose confidence. It is hard to sustain momentum when your work plan only includes goals that take many years to realize. Communities undertake housing initiatives because they have a pressing need. Long-term goals, such as adding housing units or reducing homelessness, require sustained effort over many years. Housing teams can struggle to maintain momentum and community trust without achieving early wins and consistently delivering regular accomplishments.

One-hit wonder. Community housing teams sometimes have a partnership in the works that achieves what is, for most communities, a long-term goal—a new apartment development or a developer bringing moderately priced homes for sale—when they are just beginning to implement a community housing approach. This situation might seem ideal, but achieving a significant goal without a plan for a sustained effort can lead to a one-time success rather than a comprehensive, sustained community housing approach. A housing work plan that includes a range of focus areas and action items can help sustain momentum after an early significant accomplishment.

With the strategies and insights offered in this chapter, your housing team is ready to embark on its journey. Taking the time to create a thoughtful housing work plan will set your housing team up for success. Tackling smaller goals and tasks will add up to your desired results over time. Expect a few detours, and be sure to celebrate when you reach your destinations along the way!

References

Abt Associates. (2016). *Assessing capacity with SWOT analysis.* U.S. Department of Housing and Urban Development. https://www.hudexchange.info/resource/4536/assessing-capacity-with-swot-analysis

Center for Community Health and Development. (2025). Developing an action plan. In *Community Tool Box.* University of Kansas. https://ctb.ku.edu/en/table-of-contents/structure/strategic-planning/develop-action-plans/main

Green, G. P., Haines, A., & Halebsky, S. (2000). *Building our future: A guide to community visioning* (Cooperative Extension No. G3708). University of Wisconsin, Madison. https://learningstore.extension.wisc.edu/products/building-our-future-a-guide-to-community-visioning-p231

Hopkins, R., Thomas, M., McCartney, C., & Balla, D. (2024). *The future we want: What is? What if? What next?* Transition Together.

Okubo, D. (2009). Community visioning and strategic planning. In R. Phillips & R. H. Pittman (Eds.), *An introduction to community development* (pp. 77–103). Routledge.

U.S. Economic Development Administration. (2025). *Comprehensive economic development strategy (CEDS) Content guidelines: Recommendations for creating an impactful CEDS.* https://www.eda.gov/resources/comprehensive-economic-development-strategy/content/swot-analysis

11

FOSTERING PARTNERSHIPS AND NETWORKS

Helen Keller understood the power of connecting with people to solve a problem. Her well-known quote, "Alone we can do so little. Together we can do so much," succinctly expresses the importance of working together (Helen Keller Archive, 2015). While Keller's story of overcoming adversity after becoming deaf and blind is most familiar, these often-quoted words, from one of her Vaudeville routines reflect the approach she used throughout her life. As an adult, Keller worked with an extensive network of influential leaders, disability organizations, and advocates. Through these partnerships, she changed global policies, established vocational rehabilitation programs, and increased access to education, affecting the lives of people with hearing and vision loss across the globe (American Foundation for the Blind, 2025).

Most of us have utilized our connections with people or organizations at some point. You may have sought out a neighbor for gardening advice or the proverbial cup of sugar. Perhaps you contacted a parent on your daughter's soccer team to ask about a job opening at her company. You

DOI: 10.4324/9781003520450-11

might also know that friend or family member who will never ask for help, even when it would make their life so much easier. Working on housing in your community is no different. Whether support comes from within or outside the community, partnerships and networks are critical to building housing capacity in rural and small towns. The work of community housing, like all community development initiatives, begins when people come together to tackle local problems (Theodori, 2008). Communities need outside expertise, tools, and funding to make housing changes happen. As a longtime Georgia Initiative for Community Housing (GICH) director noted, it is nearly impossible to tackle housing and neighborhood revitalization without partnerships (Tinsley & Massey, 2009).

Stronger Together: How and Why Collaboration Fuels Community Housing

The community housing approach relies on collaborative relationships within and outside the community. Rural and small towns often lack the capacity and resources to solve housing challenges. While larger cities can hire people with capacity, smaller communities must develop it. The concept of social capital helps explain why strong partnerships are key to successful housing initiatives. As you might recall from previous chapters, *social capital* is a powerful resource created through our connections to people (Brisson, 2009; Coleman, 1988; Putnam, 2001). Every community has people with valuable skills and knowledge. When these talents combine with strong local connections, they become a powerful resource for solving problems (Chaskin, 2001). Drawing on close relationships developed over time among people with similar backgrounds is known as *bonding* social capital (Granovetter, 1973; Woolcock & Narayan, 2000). Bonding social capital is often associated with rural and small towns, where people are familiar with one another and share similar networks (Claridge, 2018). Social capital embedded in close-knit ties is a key resource when you are looking for human or financial resources (volunteers or funding) to support local activities in your housing plan, like neighborhood clean-ups, windshield survey data collection, and housing fairs.

Partnerships that connect rural communities with outside expertise, knowledge, and resources also use social capital. Reaching outside the community can connect your housing team to essential information, new contacts, and unrealized options. These external connections utilize *bridging* social capital. Bridging social capital is developed through connections with people and organizations from different communities and social groups who provide access to information, expertise, or new productive connections (Granovetter, 1973; Woolcock & Narayan, 2000). Bridging social capital, which can form through internal and external connections, is associated with new opportunities and connections that help people and organizations "get ahead" (Claridge, 2018; De Souza Briggs, 1998). This type of social capital is an essential resource for a community housing initiative. The housing team model, reliant in no small part upon bridging social capital, purposely brings together people and organizations with different perspectives and expertise. In the GICH program, housing teams are encouraged to, and provided increased exposure to, build capacity and gain expertise through external connections. Some examples include:

- Learning from peer communities.
- Accessing technical assistance from housing and community development organizations.
- Partnering with colleges or universities to conduct needs assessments, facilitate community visioning sessions, or assist with community housing surveys.
- Viewing presentations and exhibitions of housing organizations, providers, or vendors.
- Touring alternative and/or exemplary housing options not extant locally or regionally.
- Meeting with government and foundations staff about potential funding opportunities.

By harnessing both bonding and bridging capital, rural and small towns can employ the conscious effort that is absolutely vital to problem-solving capacity. And while rural places have the attributes for collective problem-solving and can utilize the inherent social capital to leverage such, the lack of leadership capacity can also make the development of effective partnerships more challenging (Putnam, 2001; Warner, 2003). Thus, cultivating leadership from within the community is paramount to overcoming limitations.

The Three-Legged Stool of Partnerships

Community housing initiatives utilize three primary categories of partners—public-sector, private-sector, and mission-driven-sector. Think of partnerships like the typical stool. One leg represents the public-sector partners, steady individuals and agencies within local, state, and federal government. The second leg of the stool includes private-sector partners, reliable representatives from the business community, or other for-profit organizations. The third leg comprises our mission-driven partners, those dependable nonprofit and faith-based organizations integral to rural and small-town life. Included within each category are common interest organizations that represent the interests of and advocate on behalf of members of their sector (Berg et al., 2018). Together, the three-legged stool remains balanced: steady, reliable, and trustworthy.

Table 11.1 Community Housing Partners by Sector

Public: Local, state, and federal government entities charged with delivering public services	*Private: The wide range of for-profit businesses that create value through commerce*	*Mission Driven: Not-for-profit, non-government organizations that serve a social, civic, educational, or religious purpose*
Municipal government leadership and staff County government leadership and staff School government leadership and staff State housing finance agencies State and federal program staff Peer cities and towns Quasi-public local agencies National or statewide local government associations	Real estate agents, companies, associations Banks Homebuilders and developers Property management agents Mortgage professionals and companies Law firms Local and regional employers Chambers of Commerce Homebuilders Associations	Nonprofit housing and community development Social service organizations Churches Faith-based organizations Foundations Civic groups Neighborhood groups Colleges and universities Area Agencies on Aging

Source: Authors.

We use the metaphor of a three-legged stool because strong community housing initiatives include all three types of partnerships—public, private, and mission driven (see Table 11.1). Partnerships are iterative and will vary for different housing work plan items. The common factor is that communities employ one or more types of partners in every aspect of their housing work, and invariably encompass all three at one point or another. Working exclusively with one or even two types of partners is self-limiting, restricting the housing team's collective knowledge, impeding its ability to leverage social capital fully, and ultimately, reducing its capacity building. While there is no one correct path to travel for establishing partnerships and no predetermined combination of partners to assure success, our experience and research suggest that housing initiatives benefit when they include partners from all three sectors.

Public Sector

Public-sector partners bear the responsibility of service delivery through the provision of goods or services by government institutions or quasi-public entities to improve the quality of life, promote equity, and support economic and social development. All levels of government—local (cities and counties), state, and federal—provide some aspect of service delivery to citizens and businesses. Locally, your community may also have public entities like specialized-purpose authorities (e.g., housing authority, development authority, urban renewal authority); shared public agencies such as libraries, senior or youth centers, public transit; and perhaps quasi-independent, publicly appointed boards (e.g., a preservation commission or a community improvement district committee). Also, not to be overlooked are external public-sector partners, such as multijurisdictional collaborations, regional planning agencies, or even state legislative panels, which are increasingly important to bridge rural service challenges.

For community housing initiatives, public-sector partnerships are critical for long-term success. Local governments possess the political capital for various housing activities (Tinsley & Massey, 2009). Although the roles of city and county government vary by jurisdiction and state, policies and decisions that affect housing are local-level activities (Abt Associates & NYU Furman Center, 2026). For example, if your work plan includes the construction of new housing, local government will need to be involved if they are the utility provider, as water and sewer infrastructure are needed for most new housing developments. Local governments often own surplus property that could be repurposed to achieve housing objectives. Most importantly, local governments adopt public policy (land use plans, ordinances, regulations, guidelines, and yes, processes) that impact land use decisions and housing proposals. State and federal governments influence housing at the local level through legislative action and uniformity provisions, as well as offering technical assistance and funding.

Beyond the general government framework, your housing team might explore public partners who may be able to wield their governmental attributes in support of your housing objectives. For instance, perhaps the local housing authority can apply for housing funding sources only available through their type of agency, or your local development authority is willing to acquire land and offer a ground lease to attract a specific kind of housing investor. There are public agencies that may not be "on point" for the housing team, but they provide a service requisite to support your objective. What if your housing team attempts to facilitate an affordable housing cluster outside walking distance to a grocery store? The public transit agency may be instrumental for success. Another example is if your state requires triplexes and quadplexes to adhere to the commercial building code instead of the residential building code. The resulting expense and paucity of commercial builders make this "missing middle" housing type unworkable. Would your team be more successful broaching this issue individually with state officials or as part of a collaborative regional network of rural jurisdictions? You can see that public-sector partners are key to progress for your housing plan.

At the state and federal levels, it is easier to identify public-sector partners. Their service provision is generally more well-defined. However, as a result, they are often less flexible and, with limited resources, they typically focus upon distressed conditions (unfit buildings, unsanitary conditions, etc.), target populations (homeless, battered women, seniors/youth, released prisoners), and housing barriers (e.g., down payment programs or construction incentives). Typically, the divisions or departments addressing housing issues direct what limited resources are available to technical assistance, funding mechanisms, and program oversight. Additionally, due to the unique role in advocating and supporting local-level initiatives, we also include associations that support local governments within the public-sector category, even though they are nonprofit organizations that could also be mission-driven-sector entities. The National League of Cities and state-level organizations like the League of Cities, Municipal Associations, or Associations of County government can all be helpful partners in providing technical expertise, navigating partnerships, and supporting local-level policies for housing.

Private Sector

Private-sector partners include businesses, business professionals, and business-focused associations and groups who create value through commerce and are profit driven. Private-sector partners, their interests, and contributions vary widely by community. They can range in size, from a local independent business owner to a global corporation. Private-sector partners come to community housing initiatives from different perspectives and interests—they are affected by housing problems, they have a genuine commitment to serving the community, or as a part of a corporate social responsibility initiative (Berg et al., 2018).

Community housing initiatives commonly partner with residential real estate companies and banks. Both can be excellent data brokers, and local banks might be particularly interested in involvement as their participation in community development projects earns them credit under the Community Reinvestment Act. Financial enterprises might participate in housing fairs, a collective lending pool, or even homeowner credit score education initiatives. Your team may want to work on housing-related issues like heir's property, and a law firm or two is willing to provide pro bono support for proactive and/or reactive solutions. More community-focused, locally owned enterprises give employees hours to "spend" in support of community endeavors, and local branches of national corporations have foundations with funds that can only be accessed by communities with local affiliates. Like all effective partnerships, private-sector partners can help build expertise and capacity among your housing team while also fostering connections to resources beyond your community that will help achieve your goals.

Mission-Driven Sector

Mission-driven sector partners, sometimes called third-sector, include organizations serving social, civic, educational, or religious purposes. Partners from this sector include a wide variety of groups, including housing and social service nonprofit organizations, foundations, churches, colleges and universities, neighborhood and community groups, and associations whose mission overlaps with community housing activities. These partnerships are typically only leveraged through the use of social capital, and their participation has the potential of a distinct multiplier effect. If your housing team is able to garner the support of a mission-driven partner, not only can it influence other third-sector partners but it can also cause the participation or amplify the participation from the public and private sectors.

For example, partnering with a local food shelf organization could provide access, knowledge, and insight about the residents struggling to find housing that would otherwise take time and resources your housing team may not have. Churches increasingly utilize their land and partnerships to develop affordable housing (Myrick, 2025). They are often willing to mobilize and engage in housing stabilization programs or provide seed money for housing revitalization grants. Engaging with multistate and national nonprofits, such as Enterprise Community Partners, Housing Assistance Council, Local Initiatives Support Corporation, NeighborWorks America, can help to fill capacity and technical assistance gaps.

The Clatsop County Case: Mobilizing Public, Private, and Mission-Driven Partners to Address Housing Needs

Clatsop is a coastal county in Oregon with a strong, tourism-driven economy. Municipalities within the county have severe housing shortages and high-housing costs, factors that have made it difficult for local workers to find housing and have contributed to high rates of homelessness in the county (Carlson, 2023). In response to increasing housing problems in the county, Clatsop County formed a regional housing task force in 2022. The housing task force is a partnership between the county and local jurisdictions, health care and educational institutions, private and nonprofit developers, economic development leaders, and other community-based organizations (Clatsop County, 2025). The housing task force meets monthly to build housing capacity, including inviting peer communities to share information about their housing work, building knowledge through mini-technical assistance presentations, and working through questions about the feasibility and challenges of prospective projects (Cannon Beach, 2025).

A regional task force meeting in 2023 highlighted a pipeline of 14 affordable housing developments in the county (Cannon Beach, 2025). These projects, all within small towns, utilized partnerships. One example is a 55-unit apartment building, which opened in 2024, in Seaside, Oregon, a community with a year-round population of about 7,000. This new housing included market-rate units for the local health care providers and permanent supportive housing units for people experiencing homelessness. The project was an adaptive reuse of a former extended stay hotel purchased by CareOregon, a nonprofit community benefit organization that provides state health care coverage. The regional housing task force coordinated planning and partner engagement. The health care institution purchased the building and provided other funding for its redevelopment. State and county government partners provided funding for the project and services. A nonprofit partner is delivering services. Working together, these partners leveraged resources, skills, and expertise to add new workforce and affordable housing to the county.

Getting Started: Building a Network of Partnerships

Remember that housing teams rarely build housing. Instead, they facilitate the process and connections to make housing happen. Much of this work happens through community and public-private partnerships. Community partnerships come in various forms—an ad hoc group, a one-time event, or a long-standing relationship based on aligned goals. Public-private partnerships often involve a contractual arrangement to deliver a good (like housing development) or a service (Lavey, 2017). In our experience, much of the day-to-day work in community housing involves building and fueling community partnerships. We have outlined the types of partnerships needed in a community housing approach. First, we offer a few suggestions to get started building a network of partnerships in your community.

Take stock of your objectives and seek out mentors. Before beginning the partnership-building process, revisit your housing team's work plan goals and consider how partners might align with and advance your objectives. Consider brainstorming these questions with your housing team:

- What are we trying to accomplish?
- What do we need to get there?

- Who can help us with this objective or a specific piece of this objective?
- Who is working in this space or has an interest or mission overlap?

If you remain stuck at the starting point after pondering these questions, consider talking with other rural small towns that have successfully addressed housing challenges. Finding leaders from different communities who can serve as mentors will give you advice and ideas to help you jump-start your efforts. If you are not familiar with any communities, search the internet. We have learned of housing successes from communities across the country by simply entering a few keywords. Once you identify a community or two, reach out and ask to learn about their housing work. In our experience, community leaders are generous with their time, willing to share their lessons learned, and understand the importance of not having to reinvent the wheel repeatedly. Copying and adapting ideas that have worked in other rural small towns will save you time.

Create an inventory of prospective partners. Make a list of public, private, and mission-driven organizations whose work potentially intersects with your housing plan objectives. Think broadly when putting your list together. While organizations on your list may work in the housing field, prospective partners do not need to be involved with housing. Prospective partners might have overlapping interests. For example, employers and school districts have a vested interest in local housing. They may contribute insight into housing problems, have resources (money, land, people), or serve as a powerful political ally. Faith-based communities often have interests in affordable housing and homelessness issues, own sites (land and/or buildings) for development, and have access to volunteers. In other chapters, we mentioned the importance of involving local government with your housing team. In addition to city or county leadership, many local government departments are directly or indirectly involved with housing. Often, third-party vendors providing plan reviews or building inspection services for the local government are looking for opportunities to host educational efforts or provide seed money to fund larger opportunities that involve housing. Also of note, as infrastructure is critical for any type of development, utility providers (often located within local government) are important potential partners.

Divide and conquer. Once you have your list of potential partners, organized by your team's identified housing needs goals, look for logical ways to break up the work. For example, one GICH team decided to form three committees—an existing building committee, tasked with activities and partnerships related to the existing housing stock, a new/infill housing committee assigned activities and partnerships related to new and future housing opportunities, and a public engagement and education committee, entrusted with activities and partnerships to build awareness, education, and political will in the community. Housing teams in the GICH program often divide work into several categories, with the most common categories including outreach and education, local policies, existing housing problems, new housing development, and funding. The divide and conquer approach has the added benefit of ensuring that team members have specific roles and responsibilities.

Conduct prospect research and build relationships around overlapping interests. Once you have your list, research each organization regarding (1) the connection to specific community housing needs and goals and (2) the potential resources they contribute. First, use your human capital at the table—who and what do you already know? Your team will surprise you. If your city or county governments have a comprehensive plan, review it. Are there housing-related objectives or issues that have already been identified that overlap with yours? Look through plans of other communities of similar size and see if they have identified partners or funding sources, particularly regional, state, and national. Dive into your list of private-sector enterprises, and review their parent corporation or sister-foundation websites for corporate giving objectives that align with local housing issues. While you can do some of your work with internet research, most of the effort will involve getting out and talking with people.

The extroverts on your housing team will likely jump in and get started with enthusiasm. For the introverts out there—we, or at least one of the more reticent authors, feel your pain. Reaching out to people can be hard, especially if the people on your list are not in your network. Start with people and organizations where you have connections, even if they are in a different context. If you do not know the contact, is there someone on your housing team or your social network who can help make an introduction or accompany you? If you have no existing connections, email, follow up with a phone call, and celebrate that you are building bridging social capital!

The Benefits of Partnerships

If you are just getting started, forming many different partnerships may seem like a lot of work—and it is in the beginning. However, the benefits of working with others whose goals overlap or align with your housing team's goals are worth the investment of time. Working in collaboration with other organizations can increase your housing team's ability to (Lavey, 2017; Phillips & Pittman, 2015):

- Understand a specific problem and how it relates to the community.
- Gain access to sources of expertise, information, and knowledge that can help build your team's housing-related human capital or assist with housing plan activities.
- Provide connections and community channels to people and organizations with an interest in housing issues, including residents who may not yet have a trusting relationship with housing team members.
- Help make efficient use of available resources and avoid effort duplication.
- Support leadership development within the community.
- Mobilize financial resources—the partnerships facilitated by your housing team are instrumental in garnering funding for housing efforts (affordable housing development and funding often rely on public-private partnerships. Some partners, like public housing authorities, can open up access to additional funding resources).
- Bring about change in the local housing stock through land acquisition and the development or rehabilitation of housing.

Collaboration is key. Partnerships are essential in fostering a successful community housing program. The dual importance of bonding and bridging social capital underscores how local connections provide the groundwork for engagement, while external partnerships enhance access to crucial resources and knowledge. Partnerships offer the transformative potential of a shared approach to housing challenges, encouraging communities to harness their collective strengths. Echoing Helen Keller's wisdom, working in partnership, communities can achieve far more than they could on their own.

References

Abt Associates & NYU Furman Center. (2026). Local Housing Solutions. https://www.localhousingsolutions.org

American Foundation for the Blind. (2025). *Biography*. Helen Keller Biography. https://afb.org/about-afb/history/helen-keller/biography-and-chronology/biography

Berg, L. van den, Braun, E., & Otgaar, A. H. J. (with European Institute for Comparative Urban Research). (2018). *City and enterprise: Corporate community involvement in European and US cities*. Routledge.

Brisson, D. (2009). Testing the relationship of formal bonding, informal bonding, and formal bridging social capital on key outcomes for families in low-income neighborhoods. *The Journal of Sociology & Social Welfare*, 36(1), 167–184. https://doi.org/10.15453/0191-5096.3411

Cannon Beach. (2025). *Housing matters*. Agendas & Meeting Materials (Clatsop Regional Housing Task Force). https://www.ci.cannon-beach.or.us/planning/page/housing-matters

Carlson, C. (2023, December 27). Small Oregon town struggles with urban scale, homelessness. *Governing* (Republished from *Daily Yonder*). https://www.governing.com/urban/small-oregon-town-struggles-with-urban-scale-homelessness

Chaskin, R. J. (2001). Building community capacity: A definitional framework and case studies from a comprehensive community initiative. *Urban Affairs Review*, 36(3), 291–323. https://doi.org/10.1177/10780870122184876

Claridge, T. (2018). Functions of social capital – Bonding, bridging, linking. *Social Capital Research*. https://doi.org/10.5281/ZENODO.7993853

Clatsop County. (2025). *Clatsop county housing information and resources*. https://www.clatsop-county.gov/county/page/clatsop-county-housing-information-and-resources

Coleman, J. S. (1988). Social capital in the creation of human capital. *American Journal of Sociology*, 94, S95–S120. https://doi.org/10.1086/228943

De Souza Briggs, X. (1998). Brown kids in white suburbs: Housing mobility and the many faces of social capital. *Housing Policy Debate*, 9(1), 177–221. https://doi.org/10.1080/10511482.1998.9521290

Granovetter, M. S. (1973). The strength of weak ties. *American Journal of Sociology*, 78(6), 1360–1380. https://doi.org/10.1086/225469

Helen Keller Archive. (2015). *Script for Helen Keller and Anne Sullivan Macy's Vaudeville performances* (Filename: HK01–04_B095_F09_030_005.tif). American Foundation for the Blind; https://helenkellerarchive.afb.org/?a=p&p=helenkellerdocumentdisplay&d=A-HK01-04-B095-F09-030&

Lavey, J. (2017). The value of partnerships in community development. *Community Builders*. https://communitybuilders.org/insights/the-value-of-partnerships-in-community-development/

Myrick, W. (2025, April 15). *Faith-based housing strategies*. Georgia Initiative for Community Housing Spring Retreat, Cartersville, Georgia.

Phillips, R., & Pittman, R. H. (Eds.). (2015). *An introduction to community development* (Second edition). Routledge.

Putnam, R. D. (2001). *Bowling alone: The collapse and revival of American community* (1. Touchstone ed). Simon & Schuster [u.a.].

Theodori, G. L. (2008). Constraints to the development of community. *Community Development*, 39(2), 91–110. https://doi.org/10.1080/15575330809489733

Tinsley, K., & Massey, J. (2009). The Georgia initiative for community housing. *Housing and Society*, 36(2), 195–211. https://doi.org/10.1080/08882746.2009.11430577

Warner, M. E. (2003). Competition, cooperation, and local governance. In D. L. Brown, L. E. Swanson, & A. W. Barton (Eds.), *Challenges for rural America in the twenty-first century* (pp. 252–261). Pennsylvania State University Press.

Woolcock, M., & Narayan, D. (2000). Social capital: Implications for development theory, research, and policy. *The World Bank Research Observer*, 15(2), 225–249. https://doi.org/10.1093/wbro/15.2.225

12

BE THE SPARK IN YOUR COMMUNITY

Addressing housing issues requires recognition that business as usual will not solve problems. When the private market exclusively shoulders the responsibility of housing, challenges accrue. The profit incentive for private market developers, builders, and landlords makes it difficult to sustain affordable and adequate housing for all community members. If local economic conditions are unfavorable, private market developers and financial institutions are likely to ignore rural areas and small towns altogether. Ultimately, families and workers in the community are left with unmet housing needs. Leaving the responsibility of housing entirely to the private market may have worked at some point in the past, but it isn't working now.

If you live or work in a small town, you know housing is essential to community vitality. It does not take expert observation skills to see the impact of vacant and substandard housing, rising housing costs, or a lack of housing for downsizing elders or starter homes for young families. If you are frustrated by the housing circumstances in your community, we understand. Throughout our collective careers, we have watched housing

DOI: 10.4324/9781003520450-12

problems compound, particularly in rural areas and small towns. It is easy to feel discouraged by the enormity of the problem. Turn your frustration into action. Housing problems do not resolve themselves. Circumstances begin to improve when someone in the community decides to do something.

Your Community's Path to Community Housing

The strength of the community housing approach is in its simplicity and adaptability. While each component is important, it is a flexible blueprint rather than a rigid protocol. Your housing team may work on multiple steps simultaneously. Or it might make sense for your community to follow a slightly different order or to repeat a step if necessary. The important thing is that you take the first step onto the path.

Eureka! The community housing approach begins with the recognition that the community faces pressing housing issues. When housing concerns reach a peak, community leaders often experience a motivational spark, realizing that housing problems are negatively affecting the community. This spark is the Eureka Moment. After acknowledging housing problems, community leaders begin gathering information and building awareness among others. This process sets the stage for the community housing approach.

Catalyze teamwork. Formal working groups, known as housing teams, comprise people living or working in the community who are committed to addressing housing issues. Housing teams do the heavy lifting for community housing initiatives. They identify and prioritize housing problems, and they prepare and implement housing work plans. Ideally, the team includes a diverse group of community stakeholders, including residents who bring different experiences and perspectives about housing. Leadership or active involvement of local government is critical to sustaining the housing team.

See the story in the data. Developing a clear picture of the community enables a housing team to identify housing needs and gaps. This step in the process involves gathering data on community demographics, employment, and housing characteristics. Use the 5a framework (see Chapter 9)—access, adequacy, affordability, appropriateness, and availability—to clarify specific priority areas. Community knowledge also necessitates compiling information about available resources and potential partners.

Create a roadmap to results. Housing teams develop work plans, where ideas become action items—steps with clear and measurable goals, tasks, and activities. Strong work plans require some preliminary work. Conducting a SWOT analysis (strengths, weaknesses, opportunities, and threats) helps to identify a team's and community's collective assets and resources as well as any gaps and potential barriers. A visioning exercise also helps housing teams create a shared picture of desired results and an imagined future. In short, work plans turn a vision for housing into goals and goals into actionable steps. This process yields obtainable outcomes.

Mobilize support early and often. Establishing political will and community buy-in through coordinated leadership and clear communication is critical to the success of housing initiatives. Without sufficient political will, it is challenging to educate and engage residents at the level necessary to garner community support. Without community support, progress can be slow and falter. A thorough understanding of community values, clear messaging that speaks to these values, thoughtful and consistent communication, and listening to and addressing concerns through community engagement strategies are essential steps in mobilizing support.

Collaborate—it's key. The last part of the community housing approach may be the most important. Housing teams do not build or rehabilitate housing, nor develop neighborhoods. *Housing teams facilitate housing action.* Housing teams focus on awareness and foster synergy with those who regulate, finance, and construct housing. Through partnerships, housing teams bolster the community's housing capacity by forming connections with people and organizations that share a common interest in addressing local housing challenges. Partners exist in all sectors—public, private, and mission driven—and form a balanced three-leg stool. The well-crafted stool has one leg of public-sector partners, steady individuals and agencies in local, state, and federal government; a second leg of private-sector partners, reliable representatives from the business community or other for-profit enterprises; and a third leg of mission-driven partners, dependable nonprofit and faith-based organizations, integral and the connective tissue of the rural and small-town lifestyle. Partnerships enable teams to maximize their capacity and access additional resources to catalyze change.

The community housing approach maps the path forward. We won't tell you it is easy. Tackling housing problems that have been brewing for a long time is a substantial undertaking. We will share that addressing housing challenges is possible with the blueprint provided in this book. As evidenced by research, experience, and the shared stories of rural and small communities, change is possible. We hope that you finish this chapter knowing you can spark that change and that the benefits are worth the effort.

Small, Stubborn & Savvy: Tales of Strategic Success

Conducting research for this book involved a lot of time spent reviewing archived work plans and administrative records of past participants in the Georgia Initiative for Community Housing (GICH). The retrospective provided us with the advantage of seeing the community housing approach in action over decades. Throughout this book, we offer cautionary tales gleaned from snapshots of community housing team struggles. Revisiting past housing initiatives reminded us of standout stories—stories that have stayed with us because they capture what the community housing approach is really about.

Thomasville, a small town in southern Georgia, is one such story. Thomasville was one of the first communities to participate in the GICH program. Twenty years later, the housing team continues to meet monthly and includes some of its original members. The community housing approach is part of the city's ethos. In the early 2000s, the Thomasville housing team identified two key priorities: to develop a homeownership education program in collaboration with community partners and to eliminate substandard housing. In their first year, the team advanced these goals by gathering input on homeownership resource needs and preferences from a community survey, creating a housing resource guide, and launching a neighborhood improvement program.

Today, the neighborhood improvement program has evolved into the Thomasville Community Development Corporation, which works to enhance the quality of life and foster wealth creation in the community's underserved neighborhoods. The organization provides grants to improve and purchase homes, clear property title issues, update business facades, plan neighborhood activities, and raise funds to support infill housing development by nonprofit and local developers (Thomasville Community Development Corporation, 2025). The housing team's housing plan goal of eliminating substandard housing spurred the creation of the Thomasville-Thomas County Land Bank

Authority in 2006. The Land Bank focuses on turning vacant and abandoned properties into productive use by using the land for affordable housing and economic development (City of Thomasville, 2025). Thomasville's local government has expanded access to housing through numerous partnerships, serving as a master class in community engagement and decision-making. There have been setbacks along the way, and there are still housing challenges to tackle. However, long-term efforts using the community housing approach are visible throughout the community. New housing built in partnership with nonprofit organizations, neighborhoods with new infill housing development, and the rehabilitation and reinvestment in both housing and infrastructure in areas evidencing substandard housing conditions. This sustained effort has yielded more housing options, improved housing conditions, and a higher quality-of-life.

Several years ago, when this book was merely an idea, we reached out to Monica about the possibility of co-authoring a book on community housing initiatives. Monica, along with her mentor and a consummate citizen-leader, Judy Senft, shepherded the nascent housing team for Madison, a small town in northeast Georgia. We knew that her perspective as small-town planner and housing team leader would provide important insight. Also, Madison is one of the first communities to come to mind when thinking about GICH success stories. Madison joined the GICH program in 2014, about a decade after Thomasville. From the outset, the Madison housing team focused on developing housing leadership and using data to guide land use planning. After a series of educational sessions and a comprehensive housing assessment, the team formed three working committees, with action items focused on the existing housing stock, future land use deficits, and neighborhood engagement priorities. These committees laid the foundation for impactful initiatives and strong partnerships. Neighborhood forums revealed that residents were not leery of housing demolition as supposed, but instead wanted the city to take action on dilapidated and vacant properties. Empowered by this feedback and new resource knowledge, the team secured a series of housing rehabilitation grants exceeding $1.5 million, revitalizing nearly all 80 identified substandard homes.

Working in tandem with the local development authority, Madison's housing team also facilitated development of its first affordable senior apartments and a family-focused townhouse community. Beyond bricks and mortar, the team heavily invested in trust-building efforts that were often housing-adjacent.

They coordinated pro bono legal services to help residents create a will, providing a proactive step to avoid heir's property hurdles and the loss of generational wealth that occurs when family-owned real estate is passed down without a will. They arranged free veterinary clinics in distressed neighborhoods to help with known animal control issues. The housing team forged partnerships to host neighborhood cleanups, home repair missions, and public safety events. These collective efforts led to visible improvements in housing conditions and neighborhood stabilization, increased access to resources, and strengthened community ties. With additional foresight, Madison engaged in active succession planning, ensuring new leadership continues the pursuit of meaningful change using our blueprint for success. Today, Madison's updated work plan documents two new affordable housing developments recently completed, extending beyond the initial target area, as well as proactive planning efforts expanding into additional disinvestment areas. Their journey reflects a deep commitment to sustainable community development.

Thomasville and Madison are just a sampling of the many standout stories. From alumni of community housing initiatives in Georgia and elsewhere to communities that employed a community housing approach on their own, success stories abound. What these success stories have in common is that they all capitalized on the Eureka Moment. These communities realized early on that housing for everyone in the community was good for business and that bringing a group of stakeholders together and building political will were necessary first steps. All of these communities began their path to a community housing approach with relatively small actions—a task force meeting, a presentation for meetings with elected officials, a cookout and information fair, a survey, or neighborhood clean-up. These communities became standout stories through persistence, stubbornly continuing to work on the actions identified in the chapters of this book, despite adversity or minor setbacks. And finally, these strategic communities are committed to listening and learning about their communities to update their work plans and engage the political leaders, residents, and vital partnerships required to achieve their housing goals.

Be the Spark in Your Community

Behind every community housing success story is a person or a small group of people who took small steps. They raised a question or started a conversation about housing in their community. If you have experienced the *Eureka Moment*, you can be that person—that spark.

What might your community look like if you take the first step? Does it include new affordable senior housing apartments, a new subdivision with starter homes for first-time homebuyers, or stylish loft apartments above shops on Main Street? Maybe you envision the vacant and dilapidated eyesore down the street replaced by new infill housing? By aligning housing with community demographics, the community housing approach supports a wider range of options. By equipping residents and local government with a process to understand, plan, and respond to housing issues, the community is in a better position to address other challenges that arise. Changes to housing are likely not the only transformations you will see in your community. The community housing approach can also improve your community's capacity to solve complex problems. Engaging in the community housing *process* can change how people view their local government, community leaders, and even one another. Whether it's housing team members or residents in a community visioning session, the process brings together people who may not normally interact or share the same views. Over time, this meaningful engagement translates to stronger connections and increased trust among residents, community leaders, and local government.

APPENDIX

CASE EXAMPLE COMMUNITIES

Case example communities, presented under pseudonyms, draw on information collected through a research study. Descriptive case examples, which use actual county and municipal names, were developed from publicly available sources.

Name Used in Book	*Real Name or Pseudonym*	*Example Type*	*Sources of Information*
Bellehaven, GA	Pseudonym	Research	Case study research (2015–2020)
Clatsop County, OR	Real name	Descriptive	Publicly available sources (cited in chapter)
Foothills, GA	Pseudonym	Research	Case study research (2015–2020)
Glenwood, MN	Real name	Descriptive	Publicly available sources (cited in chapter)

(*Continued*)

Name Used in Book	*Real Name or Pseudonym*	*Example Type*	*Sources of Information*
Greenfield, GA	Pseudonym	Research	Case study research (2015–2020)
Madison, GA	Real name	Descriptive	Callahan, author and planner for Madison, GA
Pine Haven, GA	Pseudonym	Research	Case study research (2015–2020)
Stewart, GA	Pseudonym	Research	Case study research (2015–2020)
Sweetwater, GA	Pseudonym	Research	Case study research (2015–2020)
Thomasville, GA	Real name	Descriptive	Personal communication, Georgia Initiative for Community Housing documents, City of Thomasville website, news stories
Windspur, KS	Pseudonym	Research	Case study research (2024)

Case study research (2015–2020) funded by Agricultural and Food Research Initiative: Foundational Program, National Institute of Food and Agriculture, Grant No. 2015-68006-22846.

INDEX

For Product Safety Concerns and Information please contact our EU
representative GPSR@taylorandfrancis.com
Taylor & Francis Verlag GmbH, Kaufingerstraße 24, 80331 München, Germany

www.ingramcontent.com/pod-product-compliance
Ingram Content Group UK Ltd.
Pitfield, Milton Keynes, MK11 3LW, UK
UKHW020002200926
475702UK00015B/2438

* 9 7 8 1 0 3 2 8 5 9 1 2 5 *